Ngugi wa Thiong'o

MANCHESTER
UNIVERSITY PRESS

*C*ONTEMPORARY *W*ORLD *W*RITERS

SERIES EDITOR   JOHN THIEME

ALREADY PUBLISHED IN THE SERIES

Peter Carey   BRUCE WOODCOCK
Toni Morrison   JILL MATUS
Alice Munro   CORAL ANN HOWELLS
Salman Rushdie   CATHERINE CUNDY
Derek Walcott   JOHN THIEME

FORTHCOMING

Anita Desai   SHIRLEY CHEW
Kazuo Ishiguro   BARRY LEWIS
Hanif Kureishi   BART MOORE-GILBERT
Timothy Mo   ELAINE YEE LIN HO
Les Murray   STEVEN MATTHEWS
Caryl Phillips   BENEDICTE LEDENT
Wole Soyinka   ABDULRAZAK GURNAH

Ngugi wa Thiong'o

PATRICK WILLIAMS

Manchester University Press
Manchester and New York

distributed exclusively in the USA by St. Martin's Press

Published by Manchester University Press
Oxford Road, Manchester M13 9NR, UK
and Room 400, 175 Fifth Avenue, New York, NY 10010, USA
http://www.man.ac.uk/mup

Distributed exclusively in the USA by
St. Martin's Press, Inc., 175 Fifth Avenue, New York, NY 10010, USA

Distributed exclusively in Canada by
UBC Press, University of British Columbia, 6344 Memorial Road, Vancouver, BC, Canada V6T 1Z2

British Library Cataloguing-in-Publication Data
A catalogue record for this book is available from the British Library

Library of Congress Cataloging-in-Publication Data applied for

ISBN 0 7190 4730 7 *hardback*
     0 7190 4731 5 *paperback*

First published 1998
05   04   03   02   01   00   99   98   10   9   8   7   6   5   4   3   2   1

Typeset in Aldus
by Koinonia, Manchester
Printed in Great Britain
by Bell and Bain Ltd, Glasgow

For Jen, with love

Contents

Series editor's foreword

Contemporary World Writers is an innovative series of authoritative introductions to a range of culturally diverse contemporary writers from outside Britain and the United States, or from 'minority' backgrounds within Britain or the United States. In addition to providing comprehensive general introductions, books in the series also argue stimulating original theses, often but not always related to contemporary debates in post-colonial studies.

The series locates individual writers within their specific cultural contexts, while recognising that such contexts are themselves invariably a complex mixture of hybridised influences. It aims to counter tendencies to appropriate the writers discussed into the canon of English or American literature or to regard them as 'other'.

Each volume includes a chronology of the writer's life, an introductory section on formative contexts and intertexts, discussion of all the writer's major works, a bibliography of primary and secondary works and an index. Issues of racial, national and cultural identity are explored, as are gender and sexuality. Books in the series also examine writers' use of genre, particularly ways in which Western genres are adapted or subverted and 'traditional' local forms are reworked in a contemporary context.

Contemporary World Writers aims to bring together the theoretical impulse which currently dominates post-colonial studies and closely argued readings of particular authors' works, and by so doing to avoid the danger of appropriating the specifics of particular texts into the hegemony of totalising theories.

Preface

Despite his undoubted prominence in the contemporary literary field – one book blurb calls him 'the most celebrated of Africa's novelists' – Ngugi's work has for some reason not received the extended book-length treatment it both needs and deserves. Introductory studies from the late 1970s and early 1980s were not followed by the appropriate lengthy and detailed analyses, nor have the literally hundreds of articles written on him coalesced into more substantial examination. Even the exemplary bibliographical and background work done by Carole Sicherman has so far failed to stimulate any new large-scale analysis. While the present volume in no way represents the missing major work on Ngugi, it is hoped, nevertheless, that it will provide a useful introduction to his writing for a range of readers.

No one working on a writer like Ngugi could fail to be conscious of the enormous weight of published critical opinion, as well as its unbalanced nature: the fact that almost too much has been written on his early novels, and too little on the more recent. Despite that looming presence, however, I have tried as far as possible to make the book my own reading of Ngugi, rather than offer a distillation of others' work, or act as referee between competing critical positions. At the same time, I have tried throughout to give readers at least a flavour of the debates on key issues in Ngugi's writing, and, where appropriate, to engage with those debates.

The overall aim of the book is both to discuss (and to re-read) various recognised themes of Ngugi's – education, the individual and the community – as well as those aspects which are less studied, such as gender, or perhaps not studied at all, such as the operation of power. Although chapter 1 'Contexts and intertexts' provides social and historical background for Ngugi himself, he, perhaps more than any other major contemporary writer, is consistently concerned with historical, cultural and political issues in his work, and the book therefore also aims to show something of the important relation of his writing to historical events and processes both inside and outside Kenya. The focus of the book is the major works, fictional and non-fictional, which Ngugi has produced in a writing career lasting more than thirty years. Since a study of this length clearly cannot hope to cover everything Ngugi has written, or even all aspects of each chosen text, I have attempted instead to give readers a sense of how Ngugi addresses himself to certain questions of particular importance, and how his engagement with them – the ways in which he portrays them, the extent to which he is sympathetic or critical of them – shifts (or not) as his writing career progresses.

It would be very possible – indeed, in some ways nothing could be more attractive to someone working with post-colonial theory – to produce a 'difficult' theoretical reading of Ngugi's work. That sort of approach, however, hardly seemed appropriate for this book, and so the use of theory (Fanon or Said, for example, in relation to the anti-colonial or post-colonial context, or Bakhtin on theories of the novel) is kept deliberately low-key and accessible. My hope is that this will enable or encourage a wide variety of readers to engage both with Ngugi's texts and with others' interpretations of them in the production of their own.

I would like very much to thank Roger Bromley for his reading – careful and engaged as ever – of the first draft, and Stephen Chan for casting a semi-sceptical interdisciplinary eye over it. Most of all, though, my thanks go to Jen for more love and patient support than anyone (and certainly not an academic endlessly closeted with his word processor) could reasonably expect.

Chronology

1938	Ngugi born in Kamiriithu, Kiambu district, north of Nairobi.
1946	Primary education in mission school and later *karing'a* (independent Gikuyu) school.
1954	Secondary education in Alliance High School.
1959	University education at Makerere University College, Uganda.
1962	Ngugi's play *The Black Hermit* is performed at the Ugandan national theatre.
1964	Ngugi graduates from Makerere, works on the *Daily Nation* newspaper, and in the autumn goes to the University of Leeds for postgraduate study. *Weep Not, Child* is published.
1965	*The River Between* published.
1967	*A Grain of Wheat* published. Ngugi takes up post as lecturer at University College, Nairobi.
1968	*The Black Hermit* published.
1969	Ngugi resigns, and spends the next year as writer in residence at Makerere.
1970–71	Ngugi lectures at North Western University in the United States.
1971	Returns to his post at Nairobi.
1972	*Homecoming* published.
1973	Ngugi becomes the first African head of the Department of Literature at the University of Nairobi.

1975   *Secret Lives* (short stories) published.

1976   *The Trial of Dedan Kimathi* published.

1977   *Petals of Blood* published; *Ngaahika Ndeenda* performed at Kamiriithu; Ngugi arrested in December.

1978   Ngugi held without trial in Kamiti prison; released in December.

1980   *Caitaani Mutharaba'ini* and *I Will Marry When I Want* (translation of *Ngaahika Ndeenda*) published.

1981   *Writers in Politics* and *Devil on the Cross* (translation of *Caitaani Mutharaba'ini*) published.

1982   *Maitu Njugira (Mother, Sing For Me)* rehearsed – and banned – in Kenya. Ngugi forced into exile, living mainly in London. The first of his children's books, *Njamba Nene na Mbaathi i Mathagu (Njamba Nene and the Flying Bus)* published.

1983   *Barrel of a Pen* published.

1984   *Baithoora ya Njamba Nene (Njamba Nene's Pistol)* published.

1986   *Decolonising the Mind* published.

1987   *Matigari* (in Gikuyu) published.

1989   English translation of *Matigari* published.

Ngugi takes up post as Visiting Professor of English at Yale.

1992   Ngugi becomes Professor of English and Comparative Literature at New York State University.

1993   *Moving the Centre* is published.

1996   Ngugi launches Gikuyu journal *Mutiiri (The Guardian)* with his wife Njeeri.

1997   Revised version of *Writers in Politics* published.

1998   *Penpoints, Gunpoints and Dreams* published.

Contexts and intertexts

CHANGES which have occurred in literary theory and criticism since the 1970s have done much to eradicate the older critical habit of reading works of literature, particularly fiction, as if they were (thinly) veiled transcriptions of events in the author's life. This kind of move away from an over-emphasis on biography has undoubtedly been liberating for the study of literature. Nevertheless, there are certain authors whose lives – even if they are not directly transcribed or transmuted into fiction – are so intimately linked to the circumstances of the production and sometimes even the very form, of their texts, that any attempt to ignore the facts of biography would be foolish. This is certainly true of Ngugi, though what is equally important in this context is the way we could 'read' Ngugi's life as emblematic of what Kenya has gone through since the 1950s. One effect of this linkage – as we shall see in greater detail in this volume – is the emergence in Ngugi's writing, particularly the novels, of a history of Kenya in the twentieth century, focusing on the colonial, anti-colonial and post-colonial dimensions.

The circumstances of Ngugi's childhood and adolescence encapsulate a range of the most significant historical and cultural aspects of modern Kenya, and of these, we will briefly mention here the land question, education, and the struggle for independence. Ngugi was born into a large farming family, and was thus immediately caught up in the continuing process of the expropriation of Kenyan land by the British, the disintegration of rural communities which this involved, and the consequent pressures on the traditional family unit. Direct take-over of indigenous peoples' land by Europeans was always a possible, even a likely, part of the process of colonisation. In Kenya, however, the British went to great lengths – even breaking laws and agreements which they themselves had established – to secure for themselves the best land in what was to them very much 'a white man's country', i.e., one which was considered particularly congenial in terms of its climate and the possibilities for whites to do well there. In particular, the area which became known as the White Highlands was one they especially coveted, where land theft was most extensive and determined, and it was there, in the village of Kamiriithu, that Ngugi was born. The effect of British land grabbing was to turn many Kenyans – above all the Gikuyu, Ngugi's people, who lived in the White Highlands – into *ahoi*, landless tenant farmers, working for others or renting their land. Ngugi's father was one of these. To the British, this was partly an unavoidable consequence, but it was also partly deliberate policy: to the extent that Kenyans worked for a wage or became part of the money economy – rather than living off their own produce, or what they exchanged that produce for – they became subject to greater economic control by the British.

Changes such as these would be severe, if not disastrous, for many indigenous cultures. The effects were made worse for the Gikuyu because of the special, indeed spiritual, status of their relation to the land, given by God to their ancestors Gikuyu and Mumbi, as Ngugi frequently reminds readers in his early novels. The connection to the land was made physical in the shedding of blood in the rituals of circumcision and clitoridectomy undergone in adolescence. As Kenyatta points out in *Facing Mount Kenya*, the British misinterpreted the nature of Gikuyu land tenure to serve their own ends:

> The sense of private property vested in the family was so highly developed among the Gikuyu, but the form of private ownership in the Gikuyu community did not necessarily mean the exclusive use of the land by the owner, or the extorting of rents from those who wanted to

have cultivation or building rights. In other words, it was a man's pride to own a property and his enjoyment to allow collective use of such property. This sense of hospitality, which facilitated the communal use of almost everything, has been mistaken by the Europeans who misinterpret it by saying that the land was under the communal or tribal ownership, and as such the land must be *mali ya serikali*, which means Government property. Having coined this new terminology of land tenure, the British Government began to drive away the original owners of the land.[1]

Faced with the comprehensive communal disaster of dispossession and forcible relocation, it is little wonder that the main anti-colonial group in the Mau Mau period should take as its title the Kenya Land and Freedom Army, nor that, in book after book, Ngugi should return to the question of the land, and the struggle for producers and rightful owners to be able once again to control what had been theirs.

In education, Ngugi experienced the fraught relation between the indigenous African system and the imported – and imposed – Western one. According to Kenyatta, traditional Gikuyu education was informal even playful in approach, but its aims were serious. It was above all a social and cultural education, which taught the community's practices and procedures, especially the importance of interpersonal relations. Conceived of as a life-long process, its location and relevance were seen as widening and deepening – from the family to the local group to the tribe as a whole – via various stages of initiation. Set against this is the foreign formal system introduced by the British, especially the missionaries, and which figures, in one guise or another, in almost everything Ngugi has written. Despite the system's alienness and complete lack of adaptation to the Kenyan context or people's needs, the Gikuyu were quick to realise the possible benefits of Western education – even if, as Chege tells Waiyaki in *The River Between*, these amount to no more than learning the enemy's wisdom in order to use it against him.

Ngugi's primary education was in a variety of schools, run

by the Church of Scotland Mission, the government, and – most importantly – the independent Gikuyu system. The latter, again figured in its emergent state in *The River Between*, was of especial significance in terms of the re-establishing of some cultural autonomy for the Gikuyu, and of presenting children with an alternative view to that offered by government or mission schools. As Ngugi says,

> In those national [Gikuyu] schools, I was made aware of colonialism as an oppressive force, whereas in the foreign mission schools colonialism was seen as a good thing … In other words, in the national schools peasant cultures were at the centre; they were glorified or upheld, developed and perpetuated. But in the missionary schools foreign culture and foreign cultural forms of expression were glorified and used to destroy all peasant cultures.[2]

The relative success or failure of Western attempts to instil foreign ideologies in African children; the extent to which these are temporarily debilitating or permanently damaging; the ways in which they can be resisted or even overcome: these are some of the problems to which Ngugi returns on numerous occasions, and in a variety of forms, in his fiction, drama and essays.

The other early formative influence on Ngugi was the struggle for independence, especially the 'Emergency' of 1952–60, and, above all, the phase of armed resistance from 1952–56 associated with Mau Mau. Ngugi's family and village suffered in a number of ways which figure in different texts. The pointless killing of Gitogo by soldiers in *A Grain of Wheat* is precisely what happened to Ngugi's own deaf and dumb step-brother of the same name; it is also typical of the brutal treatment of innocent people during this period. The decision by the studious Njoroge's elder brother to join the Mau Mau in *Weep Not, Child* parallels the actions of Ngugi's elder brother Mwangi, which resulted in the arrest of his mother and, as Ngugi says in *Detained*, three months of torture for her at the local home guard post in Kamiriithu. The importance of Mau Mau for Ngugi as a writer and activist – and, he maintains, for Kenya as a country – has continued to grow, as even the most cursory reading of his books will make clear. It is a topic to which, like Ngugi, we shall return frequently in the course of this study.

Ironically, Ngugi was being exposed to the best and worst faces of British colonial culture simultaneously: the worst, obviously, in the shape of the bloody actions of the British and their Kenyan associates in crushing resistance, not to mention the massacres and executions which continued after the end of the fighting; the best in the shape of enlightened secondary education at Alliance High School, followed by university education at Makerere University College in Uganda, where Ngugi's specialising in English meant contact with supposedly the most 'improving' thing Western culture could offer – good literature. Ngugi read widely at Alliance, partly set texts (Shakespeare, Shaw, Tennyson, Wordsworth), and partly his own choice from the school library, ranging from Tolstoy and Dickens via Robert Louis Stevenson and Alan Paton to Rider Haggard, thrillers and the Biggles books. The reading he did served to highlight the 'best–worst' split for Ngugi, forcibly demonstrating that innocently enjoyable stories could have far-reaching political or ideological implications:

> Biggles the flying ace and squadron leader of the Royal Air Force could have been dropping bombs on my own brother in the forests of Mount Kenya. Or he could have been sent by Raymond of Scotland Yard to ferret out those who were plotting against the British Empire in Kenya. Either way he would have been pitted against my own brother who, amidst all the fighting in the forest, still found time to send messages to me to cling to education no matter what happened to him.[3]

The latter point also serves to emphasise the importance which education could retain for Kenyans, even at times of national crisis when it might well appear inessential.

From a relatively early age, Ngugi wanted to be a writer, and the styles of Dickens and Stevenson were ones he particularly wished to emulate – though in fact his earliest attempts at getting published were inspired by the thrillers of Edgar

Wallace and by Tolstoy. The latter was successful, the former not – which perhaps revealed the value of 'good' literary models. Interestingly, while at Alliance High School, Ngugi debated and won the motion that 'Western education has done more harm than good', and received a warning from the headmaster never to become a political agitator, since they were all scoundrels.

At Makerere, the process of a broadening and deepening acquaintance with literature continued, as Ngugi studied English Literature from the Anglo-Saxons to the early twentieth century, and wrote an extended essay on Conrad, whom a number of critics have discussed as a stylistic and thematic influence on his novels. As at Alliance, however, the most important textual discoveries were extra-curricular. Achebe's *Things Fall Apart* introduced Ngugi to contemporary African writing in English, while George Lamming's *In the Castle of My Skin* did the same for the Caribbean and the black diaspora generally. Lamming's work later became the subject of Ngugi's (unfinished) MA dissertation at Leeds, part of which was eventually incorporated into his first book of essays, *Homecoming*. The process of exposure to, and influence by, canonical and emergent forms of writing in English was not, as one might tend to imagine, simply one where Ngugi was first educated in a narrow, formal manner about the glories of English Literature and then subsequently made the liberating and empowering discovery of black writers. For a number of years, he continued to discover, read and appreciate both areas simultaneously.

Despite such simultaneity, however, the realisation of the presence of a number of black writers in the world outside academia, combined with their complete absence from official syllabi, had a profound effect on Ngugi. Although the gap between official and extra-curricular texts – and especially the images of the world which they represented – narrowed considerably at Leeds, and Ngugi at last received radical interpretations of them from lecturers such as the veteran Marxist scholar of English, Professor Arnold Kettle, the important discoveries and connections continued to be made outside the set texts. At a personal level, these consisted principally of contact with other

African students such as Grant Kamenju and Peter Nazareth, as well as with left-wing English ones. In textual terms, the main influence was undoubtedly the Marxist tradition: a broad range of the writings of Marx and Engels; Lenin (Ngugi declared Lenin's *Imperialism – the Highest Stage of Capitalism* 'an eye-opener'); Marxist creative writers such as Brecht and Gorky; and radical Third World writers such as Fanon and C. L. R. James. The kind of insights into the workings of colonialism and neo-colonialism offered by Fanon and Lenin were important for the development of Ngugi's thought generally, but also immediately combined to make his new novel *A Grain of Wheat*, which he was writing at Leeds, notably more politicised than the two which had preceded it.

His readings of Marx would obviously provide Ngugi with a clearer sense of the workings of the class system – analysis of which is so often absent from discussions of colonialism and neo-colonialism – as well as the ability to be able to assess how class might operate differently outside the European context which was the focus of Marx and Engels' studies. Lenin's *Imperialism – the Highest Stage of Capitalism* offered a framework which more immediately included Africa, as well as highlighting the systematic nature of European expansion, which could otherwise easily be seen as haphazard. Indeed, the deliberate, calculated side of imperialism was usually strongly denied by historians and other commentators, Sir John Seeley's much-quoted remark that the British acquired their empire 'in a fit of absence of mind' being only one of the best-known of such disclaimers. In terms of Marxist debates, Lenin's analysis of imperialism is now often regarded as somewhat dated. Ngugi nevertheless feels differently about it: 'Even today I still think that this work ought to be compulsory reading for all students of African and Third World literatures.'[4]

The relevance of Fanon was even greater, since here was someone involved in anti-colonial struggle, speaking from, and to, the Third World in a way older Marxists obviously were not. Despite the relevance, Ngugi's position on Fanon would appear to have wavered. Of his Leeds period he has said:

The political literature of Karl Marx and Frederick Engels was important and soon overshadowed Fanon. Or rather, Marx and Engels began to reveal the serious weaknesses and limitations of Fanon, especially his own *petit* bourgeois idealism that led him into a mechanical overemphasis on psychology and violence, and his inability to see the significance of the rising and growing African proletariat.[5]

One needs, however, to set that against Ngugi's frequent use of Fanon in his essays as the person who correctly assessed the negative nature of the black bourgeoisie, as well as his recent references in *Moving the Centre* to Fanon's *The Wretched of the Earth* as 'a sort of Bible' for African students at Leeds, and to the literature of the period of decolonisation as a series of imaginative footnotes to Fanon.

Another important black radical figure for Ngugi is the Caribbean-born C. L. R. James, whom he met at Makerere while James was visiting Uganda in 1969. As Ngugi says: 'If I could make every black person read one book on the history of black people in the West, that would have to be C. L. R. James's *The Black Jacobins*'[6] and many people, black and white, would no doubt agree. James's book is exemplary as an early work of radical revisionist historiography: written from a Marxist perspective, it locates its point of view close to the insurgent masses in Santo Domingo and their European counterparts in revolutionary Paris, and tells a story which historians had previously ignored or been unable to construct. An element of James's study which finds an echo in the kind of arguments Ngugi has put forward is the demonstration of the connectedness of struggles which are geographically distant from one another, in this case, the fact that the actions of the working class people of Paris had profound implications for the slaves in Santo Domingo – and vice versa – and that both of them affected what the European ruling classes did. Another important insight was the way in which new and apparently radical or progressive governments could be more than happy to continue the reactionary and oppressive policies of their predecessors – for example, the way in which the various forms of the supposedly revolutionary government in Paris failed to live up to their revolutionary slogans of *Liberté, Fraternité* and *Égalité* when it was a question of race, colonial possessions and the freeing of slaves.

James's type of approach to history is something to which Ngugi has become increasingly, passionately, committed, and which has occasioned some harsh criticism, especially from professional historians (particularly, but not exclusively, Kenyan) who clearly object to a novelist not merely trespassing on their territory but presuming to challenge their findings. As well as offering a model of intellectual practice in his radical oppositional approach to history, James stands out as someone who, despite all the vagaries of politics and vicissitudes of history in the twentieth century, retained a clear-sighted belief in left-wing politics and the possibility that ordinary people could create a fundamentally better world for themselves. In a similar way, Ngugi has, to the despair or disbelief of certain commentators, not only remained true to his radical positions but has arguably strengthened his allegiance.

Ngugi's Marxism has, at different times and in different ways, interacted with two other systems of thought and belief, the Christian and Gikuyu religions. His home background did not incline him to either religion – or indeed to religion at all: Ngugi has stated that while his parents were not converts to Christianity, they did not concern themselves much with Gikuyu religion either. By the time he got to Alliance High School, Ngugi had, on his own admission, become 'rather too serious a Christian', a fact which he later felt had stood in the way of involvement in social issues. In 1970, however, he gave a controversial talk to the annual assembly of the Presbyterian Church of East Africa (reprinted in *Homecoming* as 'Church, Culture and Politics'), where he declared: 'I am not a man of the Church. I am not even a Christian.'[7] In this talk, Ngugi presents a strong critique of the role of the Church as an institution in relation to colonialism (especially the latter's control of Kenya, its denigration of indigenous cultures, etc.) and its position in the emergent neo-colonial order. As well as urging the rejection of capitalism and greater social involvement on the part of the

Church, Ngugi also suggests a powerful form of cultural syncretism:

> If the Church in the past has been the greatest cause of the mis-shaping of African souls and cultural alienation, it must, today, work for cultural integration. It must go back to the roots of the broken African civilisation: it must examine the traditional African forms of marriage, traditional African forms of sacrifice. Why were these things meaningful and wholesome to the traditional African community? ... Can the core of Christian faith find anchor in some of these symbols, or must it be for ever clothed in the joyless, drab and dry European middle class culture? These are not idle questions: for the symbols with which we choose to identify ourselves are important in expressing the values held by a community.[8]

Ngugi also notes in the talk that, as a Kenyan African, he, like it or not, cannot escape the influence of the Church. An example of the latter's pervasiveness can be seen in his categorisation, in an interview given while he was studying at Leeds, of his writing as a process of confession – an image which is striking not least because it suggests the writer as a figure with a burden of sin or guilt which requires cleansing via the confessional process.

Throughout his writing, Ngugi shows a wide range of characters adhering to traditional Gikuyu beliefs or imported Christian ones, while others who may not be believers still invoke aspects of the religion; in addition, he draws on both systems as a source for powerful images and symbols which implicitly or explicitly comment on the action in his works. Their value for Ngugi, however, lies not in the fact that he himself believes in them, or not (despite the efforts of certain critics to claim him as a closet Christian), but in the ability of such symbols to speak to audiences both inside Africa and beyond.

During his time in England, Ngugi gained more experience of different kinds of political activism: he helped to found the Caribbean Arts Movement with writers and activists such as Andrew Salkey and John La Rose; he spoke at a writers' conference in Beirut and toured Palestinian refugee camps; he was guest of honour at an international PEN (International Association of Poets, Playwrights, Editors, Essayists and Novelists) conference in the United States. As a result, it was a more politicised Ngugi who returned to Kenya to take up a post at University College Nairobi – the first African in the English Department – and was soon involved in the first of the various 'decolonising' moves he has made. This was the famous proposal, made jointly with two colleagues, Taban Lo Liyong and Henry Owunor-Anyumba from the Department of African Studies, to abolish the English Department and replace it with a Department of African Literature and Languages. Although Ngugi's initiative has become the best-known example of its kind, it was part of a continent-wide reassessment of the role of universities and the teaching of literature in the early period of independence. In 1963, for example, there had been conferences in Senegal and Sierra Leone which brought together writers and academics to discuss these issues. In East Africa, too, the debate ranged across national boundaries. In the case of the Nairobi department, the attempt was only partly successful: changes were made to the syllabus in 1969; in 1970 the name was changed to the Department of Literature; by then, however, Ngugi had resigned in protest against increasing restrictions on academic freedom. It is important to note here that both of the central aspects – the attempt to give far greater weight and value to African culture, especially in relation to Western culture, and the refusal of the constrained position of cultural producers, academics, and intellectuals generally in the post-colonial world – are ones to which Ngugi has subsequently returned on many occasions and in many formats.

In suggesting what they did, Ngugi and his colleagues were in one sense doing no more than continuing or extending the kind of 'Africanising' proposals made earlier and elsewhere. The Senegalese poet David Diop, for instance, had written in 1956, in tones which strongly echo those of Fanon: 'The African creator, deprived of the use of his language and cut off from his people, might turn out to be only the representative of a literary trend of the conquering nation ... surely in an Africa freed from oppression it will not occur to any writer to express otherwise than in his rediscovered language his feelings and the feelings of his people.'[9] The apparent obviousness of such a process, as well as the central importance of African culture for African people, seemed to Ngugi and others to be lost on many – possibly the majority – of writers and academics.

A principal point of reference for Ngugi and his colleagues was a talk given at a conference in Makerere in 1962 by the Nigerian critic Obi Wali, in which he argued that as long as writers in Africa continued with their uncritical acceptance of European languages, it would be impossible for African culture to advance. Nevertheless, in Ngugi's case almost another decade would have elapsed before he took the 'obvious' step of writing in his own Gikuyu language, and yet another before he made his brief 'farewell to English as a medium for any of my writings' in the prefatory statement to *Decolonising the Mind.* While some might choose to see these as inconsistencies, Ngugi nevertheless continued an uninterrupted engagement with debates in history, politics and culture throughout the period. His return to the University of Nairobi Department of Literature in 1971 continued the process of syllabus modification, while his promotion to Head of Department two years later (the first African to hold the post), meant that the gains were unlikely to be reversed.

A repeated criticism of academics is that such radicalism as they may possess is usually manifested within the relatively safe confines of the institution. Similarly, would-be radical authors are accused of not being able to write for, or speak to, the people whose cause they espouse. In opposition to such criticisms, and as another stage of his Quest for Relevance, Ngugi in 1976 began working on a jointly-authored, collaboratively-produced play, written in Gikuyu and acted by ordinary people from his home village of Kamiriithu. The involvement of writers, cast and audience in the critique and revision of the play recalls Brecht's very similar strategy from the 1930s for the production of a more democratic and more radical form of theatre. In Ngugi's case, this radical cultural experiment, conducted in the 'real' world outside the walls of the university, appears to have played a greater part in his subsequent arrest and detention than the more outspoken attacks on the current regime contained in his recently published novel *Petals of Blood*. In addition, it convinced Ngugi of a number of things: the importance of writing in Gikuyu as a means of communicating with his own people; the ability of ordinary people to play an important role in the production of cultural artefacts generally supposed to be beyond their capabilities; and the power of democratically-oriented initiatives (even if not overtly 'political').

In addition to reinforcing the importance of writing in indigenous languages, his time in prison made Ngugi aware of the need both to draw on African cultural forms and to use the language and forms to create something new. As he says in *Detained*: 'I had resolved to use a language which did not have a modern novel, a challenge to myself and a way of affirming my faith in the possibilities of the languages of all the different Kenyan nationalities.'[10] As the individual chapters in this volume on works published after *Petals of Blood* make clear, Ngugi has increasingly striven to incorporate elements from Kenyan culture, above all – but not, despite what certain critics like to assert, simply or exclusively – Gikuyu culture. The most important example of that, and arguably the one with the most far-reaching consequences, was his second 'people's play', *Maitu Njugira* (*Mother, Sing For Me*). This was an even more collaborative and inclusive project than *Ngaahika Ndeenda* (*I Will Marry When I Want*), drawing, for example, on the music and songs, proverbs and stories of the major ethnic groups of Kenya, with the political importance of the need for inclusion outweighing the fact that they might not always be mutually intelligible. The rehearsals in Nairobi in 1982 were attended by thousands of people, a fact which had much to do with the government crack-down which followed, and involved banning the performances, the destruction of the Kamiriithu theatre and, ultimately, Ngugi's exile. As Ngugi said in a statement issued on behalf of the theatre group: 'It now seems, despite constitutional safeguards, that any public examination of Kenya's society, its history or future, cannot be done without raising the nervousness of the authorities.'[11] Ngugi has told the story of how in 1982 a last-minute coded message prevented his return from London, where he was promoting *Devil on the Cross*, the English translation of his first Gikuyu novel, *Caitaani Mutharaba'ini*, written in prison.[12] Return would have meant certain arrest, and ever since then Ngugi has been forced to live outside Kenya.

In addition to the plays, the search for socially relevant cultural forms led Ngugi to children's books. The first of these, *Njamba Nene na Mbaathi i Mathagu* (*Njamba Nene and the Flying Bus*), was published in 1982. As well as being written in Gikuyu, these were designed to be historically informative consciousness-raising stories about the Mau Mau period, carrying many of the same messages as his adult fiction.

While Ngugi's years of initially precarious exile in London, followed by more secure ones as Professor at Yale and New York, have been fertile in terms of his essay writing (with several collections published in this period), they have, unfortunately, been very lean years for his fiction. *Matigari*, which in some ways marks the novelistic culmination of Ngugi's turn to the history, language and central concerns of Kenya as the basis for his writing, is the only novel to emerge. There is, no doubt, a sense in which the circumstances of the semi-nomadic life he has been obliged to lead are more congenial to the production of shorter, more 'occasional', non-fiction. In this respect, it will be interesting to see whether Ngugi's latest book *Penpoints, Gunpoints and Dreams*, published in 1998, represents a text for an occasion, or a shift to a less obviously political stance. The chapters of the book were originally presented as the 1996 Clarendon Lectures at Oxford University, the sort of prestigious opportunity which seemed to elude Ngugi when he was simply an exiled Marxist living in Islington, while the tone of the discussion – surprisingly, perhaps – is more congenial to an Oxford audience than anything Ngugi has written since leaving Kenya.

Exile also raises the problem of separation from one's

people, land and culture as inspirational source. This is something which all exiled writers face, but which is particularly
acute in the case of Ngugi who was in the process of deepening
and publically articulating those very attachments. At the same
time, being permanently outside Kenya has meant that Ngugi
has functioned as even more of a public intellectual, lecturing
and speaking in all sorts of contexts and in all continents, still
most frequently from a Marxist and anti-imperialist perspective.
Given that, it comes as little surprise that the major intellectual
touchstones for Ngugi in this period remain fundamentally
unchanged: the committed artists, activists and theoreticians –
Brecht, C. L. R. James, Fanon, Cabral, Césaire, Ousmane, Alex
La Guma, Maina wa Kinyatti – articulating their opposition to
imperialism as a form of international class-based domination.

The events of Ngugi's life from 1977 onwards (arrest,
detention, harassment after release, the struggle for re-
instatement at the university, the attempt at a second people's
play, exile and involvement in expatriate oppositional politics)
on the one hand seem like an extreme version of the fate of
many post-colonial figures and on the other very much typify
Fanon's warnings about the kind of behaviour which could be
expected in the post-colonial period from indigenous black elites
in the former colonies. The slide of his country – and so much of
the continent – into conditions of neo-colonialism is undoubtedly
one of the most important factors in Ngugi's adult life, and one
with which virtually everything he has written since *A Grain of
Wheat* has in some way been concerned. To the extent that, in
retrospect, its origins are also visible in the colonial period, it
could be said to form the single over-riding theme in his entire
output, the context above all others in which his work must be
situated.

At the same time, that process has involved a struggle for,
and redistribution of, power in Kenya, and for Ngugi this is of
fundamental importance both as social and historical context,
and in the analysis of literature. As he remarked to his young
interlocutor, in connection with his own plays, in a recent
interview: 'How is power organised in that society [i.e. Kenya]?

How are wealth and power distributed in that society? How does that affect people in the areas of culture, in their psychology, in their values and how they relate to one another?[13] Accordingly, the forms of power, its distribution in society, its modes of operation, and its effects on people, will be central to the examination of Ngugi's writing in the chapters which follow. In addition, while Ngugi's Marxism would make him wary of any easy acceptance of Michel Foucault's famous dictum 'Where there is power there is resistance',[14] it is very clear that indigenous resistance to oppressive power in all its colonial and neo-colonial manifestations provides both historical and cultural context for Ngugi, as well as theme and content for his texts, and as such, analysis of power and resistance will form important aspects of the present study.

Constructing the community: narrating the nation

W HILE it has become an important insight of recent literary and cultural criticism, not least in the field of post-colonial studies, awareness of the relation of the novel and national identity is not itself a particularly recent phenomenon: Balzac, for example, felt that the novel was 'the private history of nations'. If Balzac's comment gives a useful sense of the intimacy of the relation, contemporary critics have stressed just how deep such intimate interconnection can go, and books like *Nation and Narration*[1] have begun the hitherto largely neglected task of detailed examination of the complexities involved. As mentioned in chapter 1, it is possible to read Ngugi's fictional output as an increasingly politically committed anatomising of the troubled development of twentieth-century Kenya as a nation, or at least as a nation-state – and the potentially difficult relationship between these two entities (which might at first glance appear virtually identical) will be discussed via the study of Ngugi's writing. While the idea of the novelist telling the story of his/her country might well seem an altogether straightforward or uncontentious process – and in certain periods or circumstances may well have been so – that is no longer the case for the post-colonial writer, and before turning to Ngugi's work (and at the risk of over-simplifying a range of complex theoretical and cultural debates), it is necessary to indicate just a few of the important issues involved here.

Firstly, there is the question of the 'Europeanness' of the novel form, and the concomitant problem of how well a European form could express an African national identity. Historically, the development of the novel paralleled the development of the European nation states and the colonial empires, and some critics have come to see this as more than mere temporal coincidence. Edward Said has, since the time of *Orientalism* (1978), been concerned with the links between imperialism and cultural forms (a concern which Ngugi from his more militant standpoint would share) and has increasingly come to regard these links as very far-reaching. In *Culture and Imperialism*, Said argues for 'the extraordinary formal and ideological dependence of the great French and English realist novels on the facts of Empire ...', adding, 'without Empire, I would go so far as saying, there is no European novel as we know it ...'[2] While not everyone would want to see the novel as dependent upon the Empire, the fact that it is both formally and ideologically affected by imperialism creates a problem for African and other post-colonial authors who want to work with the genre. In turn, this situation has produced a range of responses, from those writers who feel that the novel, given its history, is inevitably contaminated and that Africans should turn to other, preferably indigenous, forms, to those who argue that such contamination is not an insuperable obstacle, that the language and the form can be used in resistant or oppositional ways, reclaimed from their imperialist heritage and appropriated for African ends. Ngugi, as we shall see in more detail later, effects a kind of synthesis of these positions: retaining the novel, increasingly using it as a vehicle for anti-imperialist arguments, but at the same time moving it closer to recognisably indigenous styles of narrative construction.

A second point concerning the relation of the novel and the nation involves the recognition that national identity, rather than being something which is essentially unchanging, is in fact historically mutable, and, rather than being simply or naturally 'there', is a historical construct, constituted in particular by the (ideologically loaded) narratives which particular communities tell themselves about who and what they are. This means that novelists do not simply represent the nation, telling stories about it, but that their narratives are part of the continuing construction of national identity. The fact of the social construction or imagining of national identity also means that there is an actual or potential struggle at the level of discourse and ideology as different groups compete for their narratives of the nation to become recognised and legitimised. In the case of Ngugi, this is most visible in relation to his vision of Kenyan peoples' history, and therefore their collective identity, as one of resistance, culminating in Mau Mau, and his desire to affirm this in the face of other versions – British colonialist; official (neo-colonialist) Kenyan – which would negate it.

Ngugi's stance also exemplifies the third important point, namely the recognition (largely post-colonial) of the urgent need for actually or formerly colonised peoples to tell a different story, to narrate their identity otherwise. One of the classic formulations of this is by the Nigerian novelist Chinua Achebe: 'I would be satisfied if my novels (especially the ones set in the past) did no more than teach my readers that their past – with all its imperfections – was not one long night of savagery from which the first Europeans acting on God's behalf delivered them.'[3] This struggle over the history of the colonised has a number of aspects: it rescues Africans from the notorious legacy of Hegel's dismissal of them as 'people without a history';[4] it establishes them as inheritors of a substantial past of which they can be proud; in addition, evidence of that type of cultural heritage is vital in the construction of contemporary (national) identities. Beyond the boundaries of the post-colonial, the battle over the past has a generalised, if not universalised, relevance, of which Ngugi has become increasingly aware:

> In terms of social change, the present face of the twentieth century is a product of the struggle between two contending forces. On the one hand, imperialism which saw the elevation not simply of the non-producer but the parasitic non-producer into the dominant ruling power, not just over people from one country but over several nations, races and countries. On the other has been social revolution which for the first time in human history sought

change and often fought for power on behalf of and from the standpoint of the producer working peoples.[5]

While some might regard this as an over-simplified image of global politics (indeed, one which verges on the metaphysical in its reduction of everything to two opposing forces of good and evil), it is one to which Ngugi remains loyal, and one which for him has great explanatory power.

A final dimension of the relation between novel and national identity which needs to be mentioned here involves another meaning of representation. We have already encountered the sense in which the novelist represents the nation in terms of providing images in his/her books. At the same time, characters in those books may represent (take the place of, stand in for) the nation at a symbolic or allegorical level. The argument for the connection between individual and wider national community in this type of text has been most famously and contentiously made by Fredric Jameson:

> Third World texts, even those which are seemingly private and invested with a properly libidinal dynamic, necessarily project a political dimension in the form of national allegory: *the story of the private individual destiny is always an allegory of the embattled public Third World culture and society*.[6] (69)

Jameson has been taken to task by the Indian critic Aijaz Ahmad for, among other things, improperly universalising claims and the reduction of all Third World writing to a single model.[7] To agree with some or all of Ahmad's criticisms of Jameson does not, however, imply that *no* Third World or post-colonial texts function as national allegories, or that in no circumstances can an individual destiny be read as signifying the fate of the nation as a whole. To accept this would be to close off arbitrarily a number of useful ways of approaching Ngugi's works.

If the relation of novelistic representations and national identity, especially in the post-colonial sphere, is complex and problematic, that is perhaps just as it should be, since the things being represented – the nation and the nation-state – occupy a position which in relation to post-colonialism is even more beset with problems. As the historian Basil Davidson has argued in his recent book *The Black Man's Burden: Africa and the Curse of the Nation-State*, despite all the claims made by the colonising nations, the form in which independence was conferred on colonised peoples – nation-statehood on the European model – was generally inappropriate and frequently a positive disadvantage. As the book's subtitle makes clear, in Davidson's view the nation-state has been a 'curse' for Africa. For a long time, however, the nation-state seemed to be the ideal to which all colonised people should aspire, not simply because Europeans endlessly told them so, but because nation-statehood appeared to have brought so many benefits to European nations (such as the economic, political and military centralisation necessary to become colonisers). In addition, the rhetoric of nationhood provided one of the best means of unifying disparate groups in the anti-colonial struggle. This could be especially important because colonialism frequently forced together, in the same arbitrarily delineated territorial space, ethnic groups who might have little or no connection with one another but who were required to constitute themselves as a homogeneous nation-state. As such, the idea of the nation has acquired such significance (verging on the mystical for some) that it is almost beyond criticism as the basis for social organisation in the post-colonial world:

> Any questioning of nationalism or of the credentials of nation-statism as the only feasible route of escape had to seem very close to betrayal of the anti-colonial cause. To warn of nation-statism's likely disaster in the future of Africa, just as it had lately been in the past of Europe, was what no one, but no one anywhere, appears to have thought sensible until years later.[8]

Given the extent of his emotional and ideological investment in such concepts for their anti-colonial potential and power, it is not surprising that they show a considerable degree of persistence in Ngugi's writing. Nevertheless, while he is very capable of criticising the failings of the nation-state, there is an important sense in which his rhetorical and ideological investment has always been with people rather than institutions or structures, and above all perhaps with that hard to define but undeniably powerful category 'the people'.

In fact, despite Davidson's assertion just quoted, there were some relatively early sceptical voices, such as that of the Martinican Aimé Césaire: 'One of the values invented by the bourgeoisie in former times and launched throughout the world was *man* – and we have seen what has become of that. The other was the nation. It is a fact: the *nation* is a bourgeois phenomenon.'[9] In case there is any lingering doubt on the matter, Césaire's younger compatriot Frantz Fanon states emphatically that: 'the bourgeois phase in the history of under-developed countries is a completely useless phase.'[10]

The River Between

The 'completely useless' bourgeois phase of which Fanon is so critical has not arrived in the world of Ngugi's first novel, *The River Between*, though its components are nevertheless discernible.[11] Set in the late 1920s, it is a study of divisions within Gikuyu society, greatly exacerbated, if not originally caused, by the growing impact of British colonialism. Against the historical background of the bitter controversies over female genital mutilation as an adolescent initiation rite and the development of indigenous cultural institutions, especially schools organised and staffed by local people, the novel charts the rise and untimely fall of the young teacher Waiyaki, partly as a result of a power struggle he both underestimates and misunderstands, and partly as a result of his love for Nyambura, daughter of Joshua, the leader of the Christian converts in their community. The struggle is symbolised in the geographical division of the community into two 'ridges', separated by the Honia river, 'which faced each other like two rivals ready to come to blows in a life and death struggle for the leadership of this isolated region' (1), and crystallises along lines of opposing religions (Christian enlightenment versus pagan savagery), attitudes to the tribe (especially in terms of betrayal versus fidelity), and social orientation (Western-oriented modernity versus indigenous adherence to tradition). The geographical separation, historical rivalry and growing contemporary antagonism between the ridges of Kameno and Makuyu is paradigmatic of the novel's organisation, both thematic and structural, around pairs of opposites: communities, cultures, groups, individuals, genders, spiritual beliefs, political tendencies and social projects. One of the major issues which the book addresses is whether, how far, and by what means these can be reconciled. There is also the relation between oppositions which are 'real' or natural (such as that between Kameno and Makuyu) and those which are manufactured or self-interested (such as that between Kabonyi and Waiyaki) – though in the end the opposition apparently solidly grounded in geographical reality and that visibly concocted for unfair personal advancement may be equally spurious (or real).

As an account of the way in which colonialism exerts pressures that can destroy traditional societies, *The River Between* has strong affinities with Achebe's *Things Fall Apart*, published six years earlier. Also like Achebe, Ngugi is concerned to counter dominant colonialist representations of Africans in general, and his own Gikuyu people in particular. In this, his novelistic practice forms a counterpart to Kenyatta's classic ethnographic study of the Gikuyu published in 1938, *Facing Mount Kenya*, in terms of revealing cultural complexity and social organisation where the colonialists would typically see mere primitiveness – or worse. The 1903 Report by Sir Charles Eliot, Commissioner for the East African Protectorate, provides a typical encapsulation of the official ideological stance with which colonised peoples had to contend – and which has not necessarily disappeared in the post-colonial era:

> Firstly, modern East Africa is the greatest philanthropic achievement of the later nineteenth century ... I do not

say that the natives admire our good deeds as much as we admire them ourselves ... But there can be no doubt of the immense progress made in rendering the civilisation of the African at least possible, and it is a progress which need occasion no regrets, for we are not destroying any old or interesting systems but simply introducing order into blank, uninteresting, brutal barbarism ...[12]

Again like *Things Fall Apart*, *The River Between* in both formal and linguistic terms is simple and straightforward, though it does not convey the same sense of an attempt to recreate a traditional mode of oral narrative which characterises the earlier novel.

At the point in the 1920s in which the novel is set, the power of colonialism is visible in what Gramsci would call a 'hegemonic mode' (aimed at winning people over, convincing them that you have their interests at heart, gaining their adherence) rather than a 'coercive' (especially military) mode. This in itself is unusual in the Kenyan context, where the preferred British method tended to be coercion, particularly in the first instance. As Sir Arthur Hardinge, first Commissioner for Kenya put it (in a sort of colonial variation on 'shoot first; ask questions afterwards'): 'These people must learn submission by bullets – it's the only school; after that you may begin more modern and humane methods of education.'[13] Talking of the early period of colonialism, Berman and Lonsdale comment: 'The British employed violence on a locally unprecedented scale, with unprecedented singleness of mind. Their external force redefined internal power.'[14] It is the latter point which is of particular interest in the world of *The River Between*.

The hegemonic struggle for the 'hearts and minds' of the Gikuyu is conducted principally through schools and, more importantly, Christian missions. As material institutions the latter have only reached the borders of the Gikuyu's territory, but disruptive practices have already penetrated deep into the community, and the effect on Joshua is an important dimension of the redefinition of internal power in this community. Joshua's conversion to Christianity, which seals the antagonism between the groups centred on the ridges of Kameno and Makuyu, is explained very much as a question of power:

> In Siriana he found a sanctuary and the white man's power and magic ... The new faith worked in him till it came to possess him wholly ... He turned to and felt the deep presence of the one God. Had he not given the white men power over all? (33)

Joshua hopes for the power of the white man's order to work through him, and in this way becomes a classic indigenous intermediary, serving as a conduit for one of the central forms of colonial control, believing that in some sense he holds power but in fact acting as a means of its deployment against his own people.

The mention of the contest for leadership on the first page of the novel is significant, not merely in terms of the world of *The River Between*, where it forms the nub of the power struggle which destroys Waiyaki, but also because leadership is a problem which recurs in different guises and with different emphases throughout Ngugi's writing, just as it does in colonial and postcolonial Kenya. At a common-sense level, leadership obviously involves forms of power, but that could be understood and exploited very differently by Kenyans or British colonialists. Part of the problem represented in *The River Between* concerns the different understandings of leadership, and the different requirements which different constituencies make of their leaders, as well as the sometimes bitter struggles to achieve the position of power and pre-eminence which leadership implies.

Gikuyu society, like any other, produces its significant individuals, and early in the novel we encounter the trait which is typical both of Ngugi and the traditional oral culture he is representing here: the listing of important individuals as a historical record of communal achievements. Here also, their naming is to advance the claims of Kameno to superiority over Makuyu. They include the Gikuyu seer Mugo wa Kibiro whose prophecy plays such an important role in the events of the novel, the magic worker Kamiri and the warrior Wachiori.

Important as these 'heroes and leaders' may be, they are not leaders in the sense of rulers; rather they are 'the select few sent by Murungu [God] to save a people in their hour of need', (3) and part of the novel's plot hinges on whether or not Waiyaki is another of these – arguably the most important, if in fact he is the one prophesied by Mugo wa Kibiro (and certainly his community is facing a situation of great need).

Another, antagonistic, conception of leadership is at work in the novel; one which derives from the actions of the British colonialists. It was normal practice for British colonialism to function with the help of indigenous intermediaries (or collaborators, if that word can have anything other than a completely pejorative meaning). Where these did not naturally or readily exist, they had to be created, or even invented, and a standard invention was the tribal chief. How far it was the case that the British always ignorantly assumed that Africans lived in tribes, and that tribes should have chiefs (otherwise they're not even being primitive properly), or how far it was a pragmatic calculation that colonialism would function more smoothly and efficiently with the help of a local intermediary who wielded authority (if not always power) is a matter of debate. In areas as far apart as Nigeria and Kenya, the British created, and imposed, chiefs where none existed: 'Everywhere else [i.e. other than some Luo and Luyia areas of Kenya] chiefship was a figment of the ethnographic imagination of the early British officials.'[15]

Chiefs were not the only intermediaries, nor was the role of the chief the only form which leadership could take, as the character of Joshua shows. If the figure of the chief embodies a (potentially) coercive type of power, then religious leaders like Joshua work very much in the realm of the hegemonic. Because the British colonial apparatus has not penetrated as far as the Kameno/Makuyu community, no chief has been forcibly installed, and it is left to Joshua to instantiate the colonialists' preferred model of leadership. Apart from the alien conception of such roles, they are also visibly predicated far more on personal prestige and power than those other leaders who are acting for the good of the community.

Although he does not comment specifically on this, such an opposition of British-oriented/self-seeking/individualism versus Gikuyu-oriented/unselfish/community-mindedness is certainly in keeping with Ngugi's view of the nature and behaviour of those who collaborated. In *The River Between* the situation is rendered more ironically complex by the fact that – to the extent that the struggle for leadership is represented by Joshua and Kabonyi (the leader of the Kiama, the newly-formed but traditionalist council) – it is a struggle between two men concerned above all with their personal power. This type of attitude in Kabonyi is less surprising when we recall that he was one of the original converts to Christianity along with Joshua, but has since returned to the traditionalist fold.

The focus for the examination of leadership in the novel is of course Waiyaki. This in itself is an interesting choice of name in view of Ngugi's strategy of including historical characters in his novels, or at least naming them, since the original, historical Waiyaki wa Hiinga was one of the early leaders of resistance to the British, and as such figures in the naming and remembering process of almost every other Ngugi novel. In *The River Between* he is not mentioned, which raises the question of whether, or to what extent, the fictional Waiyaki is meant deliberately to evoke and represent his real life predecessor (the fact that his father is called Chege, another name by which Waiyaki wa Hiinga was known, is obviously no coincidence). Both Waiyakis – the fictional very clearly, the historical to a lesser extent – represent problematic aspects of leadership, or even the leader as problem. Leadership is problematic for the individual because of the physical risks involved (of the three mentioned at the start of the novel, two are killed and the third disappears), because they are frequently undervalued by the community (the great seer Mugo wa Kibiro, for example, is simply not listened to), and because it is also alienating (the three mentioned by Ngugi become strangers to their own people, to the community they have helped save). Leadership is also problematic for the community, because of the power which they may delegate, or which the leader may arrogate to himself, and because so many of the leaders seem to fail in one way or another – and the figure of the leader who fails, disappoints or betrays his people haunts a great deal of Ngugi's writing.

One version of the story of the historical Waiyaki emphasises his championing of non-violent methods of resistance, and this is also the approach adopted by his fictional counterpart. To that extent, both disappoint or antagonise sections of their community. While Waiyaki's misjudgement in *The River Between* does not directly cause his downfall, it is indicative of the (ultimately fatal) way in which he loses touch with his people. In terms of organising the resistance of the community, Waiyaki has mixed success – he strengthens the potential for passive resistance, via cultural self-confidence, for example, but neglects the more active, political, physical, or even armed options, which are favoured by the Kiama and would also be in keeping with the traditions of the community. Such an approach typifies both his personal preferences and the cultural syncretism which he embodies.

One important function of the leader is to act as a focus of power and the means of its beneficial deployment. Waiyaki combines spiritual power (as the possible saviour prophesied by Mugo wa Kibiro), the power of knowledge (his father Chege sends him to the elite Siriana school to imbibe the white man's knowledge and power, as a means of being better able to resist colonialist incursions), the delegated power of the community (they increasingly push him into a position of leadership beyond what he had aspired to), and the power of his own personality (his vision, personal charisma, rhetorical skills, ability to inspire and organise, etc.). The deployment of this power is very focused and for a time, very successful. Waiyaki's aim is to rebuild and eventually reunite the divided community. His immediate strategy is to start Gikuyu-run schools to provide both education and a focus for cultural pride for the community. The impetus created leads to the formation of the Kiama, which embodies a more obvious and traditional form of power, and which Kabonyi aims to dominate and use as a means to defeat Waiyaki. In terms of starting schools and rebuilding the confidence of the community, Waiyaki achieves a lot; in terms of uniting the community, he appears to fail comprehensively, his failure coming precisely as a result of the clash between the purist, nativist or conservative cultural attitudes embodied in the Kiama, and his own syncretic or synthesising approach. Waiyaki's love for Nyambura, which at one level is the personification of the reconciliation of the two warring groups in the community, ironically leaves him open to a range of accusations. These include *thahu* or ritual uncleanness (brought about by contact with an uncircumcised woman), and consorting with the enemy (the 'traitor' Joshua and the Christians; perhaps also with the white men – which in fact Waiyaki has not done), and as a result, of betraying his oath to the tribe.

One final point to make regarding leadership at this stage is its messianic dimension. Clearly, that has relevance for Waiyaki, given Mugo wa Kibiro's prophecy (and his own descent from Mugo). While he remains unsure whether in fact he can possibly be the one foretold, others have fewer reservations about seeing him as their individual or collective saviour: 'She could only be saved through Waiyaki. Waiyaki was then her Saviour, her black Messiah, the promised one who would come and lead her into the light'(117). Nyambura's conflation of her feelings towards Christ and those she has for Waiyaki is one sign of the rapid indigenous assimilation and appropriation of Christian discourse, though references to the figure of a black Messiah or black Moses in Ngugi's work usually have collective rather than individual resonance.

The ability of individuals to see themselves as the saviours of their people, even in the total absence of any supporting evidence, is widespread, if not endemic, in Ngugi's writing. In *The River Between* there is at least the prophecy, and though Chege wonders whether his ancestor's words might apply to him, he feels that the mantle properly falls on Waiyaki. Also, part of the reason for Kabonyi's hatred of Waiyaki is that he wants to be the prophesied saviour, and cannot bear the thought that it might be his rival Waiyaki – even though he rationalises it otherwise:

To him, then, this was not a personal struggle. It was a
continuation of that struggle that had always existed
between Makuyu and Kameno. For leaders from Kameno
had failed, they had only betrayed people. The ridges
would now rise and cry vengeance. Kabonyi felt himself
the instrument of that vengeance. He was the saviour for
whom the people waited. Not that Kabonyi knew exactly
where he would lead the people. (166)

In the struggle between Kabonyi and Waiyaki, which is almost
one-sided for as long as the latter fails to realise that there *is* a
struggle, it is not simply about who will lead the community,
but also about what sort of community they will lead. This in
turn involves the deliberate construction of something which is
still experienced as natural and organic, while the construction
of this more localised community has implications for the later
and larger anti-colonial and post-colonial projects of constructing the national community. In common with the organicist
image, a community of this size would, in theory, be knowable
by all its members, and therefore could arguably be grounded in
a 'real' image of the community, in a way which is not available
to members of the 'imagined community' of the nation.
However, the situation is not clear-cut, as Anderson points out:

In fact, all communities larger than primordial villages of
face-to-face contact (and perhaps even these) are imagined.
Communities are to be distinguished not by their falsity
or genuineness, but by the style in which they are
imagined.[16]

Waiyaki and Kabonyi clearly imagine their communities in
ways which contrast and can be made to conflict. At its simplest,
this rests on an opposition between, on the one hand Kabonyi's
nativist or traditionalist model predicated on strict adherence to
tribal custom and the maintenance of cultural purity, and on the
other Waiyaki's belief in the combinatory potential of cultures:

For Waiyaki knew that not all the ways of the white man
were bad. Even his religion was not essentially bad. Some
good, some truths shone through it. But the religion, the

faith, needed washing, cleaning away all the dirt, leaving only the eternal. And that eternal that was the truth had to be reconciled to the traditions of the people. A people's traditions could not be swept away overnight. That way lay disintegration. Such a tribe would have no roots, for a people's roots were in their traditions going back to the past, the very beginning. (162)

While Waiyaki's position arguably lacks a properly historical sense of the way in which, in the words of Hobsbawm and Ranger, traditions are invented (in ways that are very similar to those national or cultural identities of which they are a significant component), it nevertheless demonstrates a useful appropriative attitude to cultural mixing.[17] Rather than merely passively accepting the alien element (here, Christianity) the community will take it, extract what is worthwhile, and mould it in ways which fit the needs of the people – and their pre-existing cultural traditions.

The same active appropriation of useful aspects of Western culture is evident in the establishing of Gikuyu-run schools to Africanise formal education:

And there they stood, symbols of people's thirst for the white man's secret magic and power. Few wanted to live the white man's way, but all wanted this thing, this magic. This work of building together was a tribute to the tribe's way of co-operation. It was a determination to have something of their own making, fired by their own imagination. (79)

Although the text sets up the somewhat polarised opposition between cultural purism (Kabonyi) and syncretism (Waiyaki), in fact many of the characters demonstrate more or less syncretic or synthesising approaches to culture (though these may sometimes appear as contradictions): Chege is a traditionalist, but sends his son to encounter 'progress' at the British school; Joshua is allied with modernity in the shape of Christianity and colonialism, but is the most reactionary of patriarchs; Nyambura and her sister Muthoni, like 'the people' in the previous quotation, want some kind of blend of the benefits of

Western and African spirituality; Kabonyi demands tribal purity, but his earlier conversion to Christianity makes him one of the most contaminated members of the community (a fact which he and the text do their best to forget about).

The cultural tradition which is the most contentious, and which is the focus for animosity between Makuyu and Kameno, Christians and 'pagans', occurs in the field of gender relations. Female genital mutilation (most frequently, and incorrectly, referred to as circumcision) was the traditional adolescent rite of passage for the Gikuyu. It also became a paradigm case of the maintenance/defence of cultural practices as a site of resistance to colonialism. The renewal in 1928 of the campaign by Church of Scotland Mission members to have female genital mutilation eradicated, and which forms the historical background to *The River Between*, looks on the face of it to be yet another British colonial attempt at stamping out indigenous practices of which they did not approve (the obvious parallel would be the banning of *sati* in nineteenth-century India). One effect of this campaign was the establishing of Gikuyu-run schools, partly because pupils being educated at the mission schools withdrew *en masse* in protest – a fact which the novel does not make clear. Although the practice was portrayed as the essence of primitive savagery and the patriarchal abuse of women's bodies, such an attitude required a degree of historical amnesia, as well as racism, since the more localised form of genital mutilation, clitoridectomy, had been practised in late Victorian England, and on a rather more widespread basis in the United States. The Gikuyu version involved cutting off the labia as well as the clitoris though Kenyatta insists that only clitoridectomy was involved, and that excision of the labia was an aberration, creating a mistaken impression among whites.

As Berman and Lonsdale suggest, the crisis occurred in part because while mission doctors had, as a result of Gikuyu pressure, eventually agreed to supervise male circumcision (and hence control it within a Christian environment), they refused – after a brief trial period – any equivalent involvement in female genital mutilation. However, far from constituting a unified colonialist assault on a united indigenous population, the issue produced divisions among colonisers and colonised alike. For Joshua (unsurprisingly) female genital mutilation is 'evil'; for Chege, on the other hand, it represents 'all that which was good and beautiful in the tribe. Circumcision was the central rite in the Gikuyu way of life. Who had ever heard of a girl that was not circumcised? Who would ever pay cows and goats for such a girl?' (44). Chege's view of the central importance of genital mutilation is echoed by Kenyatta in *Facing Mount Kenya*: 'It is important to note that the moral code of the tribe is bound up with this custom, and that it symbolises the unification of the whole tribal organisation.'[18] For Waiyaki, the importance rests on the changes which it brings about inside a person, and he also agrees with Kenyatta that change must come about gradually, especially via education, rather than abruptly, via legislation. The narrative voice states:

> Circumcision was an important ritual to the tribe. It kept the people together, bound the tribe. It was at the core of the social structure, and something that gave meaning to a man's life. End the custom and the spiritual basis of the tribe's cohesion and integration would be no more. (79)

In her article 'The Master's Dance to the Master's Voice' on the representation of women in Ngugi's novels, Elleke Boehmer suggests that the sisters Nyambura and Muthoni can be seen as potential Mumbis (the strong central female character from *A Grain of Wheat*), and 'like Mumbi, are consistently viewed in their relation to men ... Nyambura and Muthoni for their part passively represent the two sides of a conflict over female circumcision directed solely by men.'[19] Even though Ngugi's representation of gender roles and relations has not achieved its later complexity at this stage, it nevertheless seems a harsh judgement to regard the sisters as entirely passive. In fact, both are capable of surprising acts of self-assertion and defiance of the patriarchal order. In particular, Muthoni's decision to undergo genital mutilation flies in the face of both Christian patriarchy and the community's rules which would enforce obedience to the will of the father. 'Muthoni's revolt had rung from hill to hill, as if the news were passed by the wind and the drums. Her name was whispered from hearth to hearth' (46–7). In addition, she has done something which not only transgresses the bound-aries of permissible female behaviour but which also constitutes a greater revolt than Waiyaki can contemplate: 'The idea that she had actually run away, actually rebelled against authority, somehow shocked him. He himself would not have dared to disobey Chege. At least he could not see himself doing so' (47). While this no doubt says much about the limitations of Waiyaki, it nevertheless remains a good guide to the enormity of what Muthoni has done.

For her part, Nyambura decides not to follow her sister, but she, too, is able to defy her father and face the antagonism of both (male-controlled) sections of the divided community – though the fact that she is empowered to do these things because of her love for Waiyaki may perhaps be taken as an indication of an ability to act only in relation to men or the dictates of patriarchal ideology. We could also, for example, read Muthoni's choice of action as defying one patriarchal system in the name of another, in which case autonomous female agency would be an illusion. A similar reading of female agency as ideologically trapped could be made of the historical events surrounding the genital mutilation debate: when in 1929 a group of male Anglican converts decided to ban the practice, their wives defied them and pressed for its retention – their actions arguably motivated as much by strongly internalised patriarchy as by anything which could be construed as autonomous agency. Elleke Boehmer argues that Muthoni is able to die happy because she has followed 'the ancient laws of the elders, the fathers of the village', whereas her dying words in fact stress her reconciling of these laws and the new Christian ones: 'Tell Nyambura I see Jesus. And I am a woman, beautiful in the tribe' (61) – though whether such reconciliation also involves submission is a difficult question.[20] Something of the same complexity surrounds Nyambura: her ability to stand up to her father who is making Waiyaki look both weak and passive in their final confrontation suggests that she is neither of these things; at the same time, her decision to go with Waiyaki despite his weakness could be read as defying patriarchal ideology only to submit to the ideology (and subordinations) of romantic love. The romantic love strand of the novel provides the climax of the plot, though it has hitherto functioned as sub-plot (and rightly so, since it is one of the weaker elements of the book). If Nyambura, as mentioned, risks confusing Christ and Waiyaki – not least as objects of adoration – then Waiyaki does his best to return the compliment, in more muted but still mystical terms, for example imagining them together at the altar – but an altar of sacrifice. This could be seen as prophetic on his part: Ngugi's first version of the novel ended with the deaths of the couple at the hands of the Kiama, and some critics have convinced themselves that this is also what happens in the published version.

Whether, finally, the women in *The River Between* are passive or not, it is certainly the case that the sphere of gender relations in the novel is one of unequal power, and the question arises whether Ngugi's representation of this state of affairs critiques or in any way endorses the inequality. It is, of course, possible to argue that Ngugi, in portraying potential female passivity or disempowerment, is merely reflecting the state of Gikuyu society at the time (an argument similar to that which critics have advanced in defence of *Things Fall Apart*). It could also be pointed out that Ngugi's thinking on the matter has changed, and twenty years later he is much clearer:

> I now believe that the oppressive reactionary tendencies in our pre-colonial peasant cultures are only slightly less grave than the racist colonial culture of fear and silence and should be fought, maybe with different weapons, but fought all the same.[21]

Ngugi does not say precisely which oppressive reactionary tendencies he has in mind, but immediately prior to the passage quoted he had been discussing the awful power imbalance between adults and children, and it is difficult to imagine that he would not include the power imbalance between the sexes as one of these tendencies.

The idea of female agency leads on to the larger issue of indigenous agency in general. The notion of black people taking an active, even progressive, role in the determining of their own history is one which both colonial historiography and an earlier generation of critics have tended to ignore, the former finding it ideologically difficult to admit of such a thing, the latter more concerned with black people as the victims of colonialism, or at least with colonialism's effects on the colonised, rather than the latter's response to it. Black agency is, however, something which even contemporary black critics can overlook:

> If he [the colonised individual] chooses conservatively and remains loyal to his indigenous culture, then he opts to stay in a calcified society, whose developmental momentum has been checked by colonisation. If, however, the colonised person chooses assimilation, then he is trapped in a form of historical catalepsy because colonial education severs him from his own past and replaces it with the study of the coloniser's past. Thus deprived of his own culture and prevented from participating in that of the coloniser, the native loses his sense of historical direction and soon his initiative as well. The limited choice of either petrification or catalepsy is imposed on the African by the colonial situation.[22]

JanMohamed's point is forcefully argued, but the omission of any sense of resistance or agency on the part of the colonised is remarkable. *The River Between* is very far from being Ngugi's most politicised work, nor is it necessarily the best exemplification of this point. Nevertheless, even at such an early stage in his writing career we can see a representation of colonised people moving beyond the apparently inescapable poles of 'petrification or catalepsy' into forms of cultural activity and anti-colonial resistance.

Although *The River Between* may offer a generalised representation of African people's agency, the precise location, form and direction of that agency may be more problematic. On the one hand, Waiyaki seems to embody, and to inspire in others, a historically specific form of cultural agency and (partial) resistance to colonialism. On the other, he can appear to some commentators as the embodiment of a repeated refusal of agency. In a highly critical assessment, Ato Sekyi-Otu says:

> Could it be that in the shifting vicissitudes of Waiyaki's life as acquiescent son of Chege, model pupil of the mission school, as man of the people, or as star-crossed lover and martyr, we may discern an invariant existential habit – one which recurrently refuses the temptation of moral agency, the 'practice of action' and the colliding obligations it occasions, preferring instead a relation to the world which is intuitive, divinatory, unitarian and non-voluntaristic.[23]

Sekyi-Otu's article appears torn between reading Waiyaki as a failed individual (tragic or not on that level) and as an intimation of something larger:

> The traditional and the modern thus conspire to spell the *combined underdevelopment* of Waiyaki's critical, oppositional and originative powers. We have here the prototypical physiognomy of petit bourgeois being and consciousness – the symptoms and pathogenesis of which Frantz Fanon unveiled with unsurpassable perspicacity – in its educated pusillanimity, its reverential (because referential) positivism, its unexamined dutifulness, and, as we shall presently see, its neutralist cult of mindless and purposeless reconciliation.[24]

As mentioned at the beginning of this discussion of *The River Between*, the emergence and development of the indigenous bourgeoisie (*petit* and otherwise) is something we shall trace through Ngugi's works. For the moment, however, it is worth noting in Sekyi-Otu's article the image of Waiyaki as the product of certain social forces, rather than individual fallibility. We could also query whether – regardless of its ultimate success or failure – Waiyaki's strategy of reconciliation, far from being 'mindless and purposeless', is not a conscious search for a better foundation for social, cultural and political power at a time when it is much needed by the community in the midst of a (necessary, if unlooked-for) process of reorganisation. The fact that Waiyaki does not quite get it right – though he is arguably getting there by the end of the novel, given his belated realisation that there has to be a political dimension to the processes under way – does not alter the fundamental urgency, in the novel's own terms, for the reconciliation of the antagonistic principles and forces at work in the community.

At the end, Waiyaki's plan for communal reconstruction and regeneration remains unfulfilled, and he leaves the community at least as divided as before. Having represented the first appearance in Ngugi's work of the intellectual as leader, Waiyaki now becomes the first representative of a more deeply problematic figure, not just in terms of Ngugi's writing, but also, and much more unfortunately, in the history of modern Kenya: the failed leader. Although he has set in motion certain progressive projects, Waiyaki has also presided over the emergence of a new dispensation of power in the shape of cultural nationalism. From the standpoint of the 1920s and 30s, and in terms of anti-colonial agitation, cultural nationalism represents the future for Kenya, with the growth of organisations such as the East Africa Association led by Harry Thuku, and even more importantly, the Kikuyu Central Association (KCA), of which Kenyatta became general secretary in 1928, the year in which the female genital mutilation controversy re-emerged. While cultural nationalism is by no means inherently regressive, it certainly has that possibility, and in the hands of a character like Kabonyi it seems destined to be so, and in that respect, Waiyaki's failure appears to condemn his people to a future under the sway of unenlightened traditionalism. At the same time, and more positively, the community has seen (well before the realisation strikes Waiyaki) the need for political action in defence of cultural and community identity – even though, once again, this initiative is likely to come under the control of the Kabonyi-led Kiama.

The future organisation of the community may be broadly democratic (Waiyaki's model) or more narrowly oligarchic, if not despotic, depending on whether Kabonyi succeeds in centralising power in the Kiama, or entirely in his own hands.

This obviously remains hypothetical with regard to *The River Between* (if somewhat less so in the context of Ngugi's perspective on Kenyan history). In terms of Ngugi's questions regarding the distribution of power in society (referred to in Contexts and Intertexts), the traditional conception of community would accord great, possibly ultimate, power to the popular will, especially as expressed in 'the voice of the people'. The problem now is that the Kiama has taken it upon itself to speak on behalf of the whole community. As Waiyaki's mother says: 'Fear the voice of the Kiama. It is the voice of the people. When the breath of the people turns against you, it is the greatest curse you can ever get' (141). This image of discourse as (social) power is important not simply as a recognition of the way in which Gikuyu society, along with many others in Africa, functioned, but also because it has relevance for the operations of power in any society. In so far as it represents a consensually-derived expression of communal will (and power) 'the voice of the people' cannot be univocal, still less what Mikhail Bakhtin would call monologic.[25] Waiyaki's attempt to give due weight or value to competing voices within the overall discursive field might be read as a suspect, liberal-pluralist type of approach; it could equally be seen as something more approximating a recognition of social polyphony or heteroglossia. One of the problems which Kabonyi represents is his determination to impose a monologic regime where his discourse, his meanings or interpretations of events, will dominate 'the voice of the people'.

The relation of discursive power and social power for the Gikuyu is made clearer by the position of the historical Waiyaki and his contemporaries such as Kinyanjui: 'They were all local spokesmen or *athamaki*, the nearest any Kikuyu approached to chiefship.'[26] While 'spokesman' may not sound like a position of particular power, *athamaki* actually translates as 'big men' and 'those who can speak', giving a rather Foucauldian picture of those who are empowered to speak, and who through their speech acquire more power: 'They conveyed an impression of a social order under their control, the asset that made their alliance worth having.'[27] In turn, the ability of leaders like

Waiyaki to represent their community (both speak on its behalf, and describe it as under their control) reinforced their power as they formed alliances with the British. Lonsdale says: 'I cannot prove historically my theoretical assumption, that Kikuyu spokesmen competed for a constantly reformulated intellectual hegemony.'[28] Despite that, just such a struggle over the forms and languages of power is fleshed out in the narrative space of *The River Between*.

The usurping of the voice of the people which Kabonyi aims for (and which indeed appears to have some historical precedent in Berman and Lonsdale's account) seems a long way from the delicate dialogical and dialectical relation of leader and community which Waiyaki expounds (the extent to which he follows his own precepts being a matter for debate): 'Waiyaki told them that he was their son. They were *all* his parents. He did not want to lead. The elders were there to guide and lead the youth. And the youth had to listen ... He, Waiyaki, would listen. All he wanted was to serve the ridges, to serve the hills' (110). This might seem no more than telling his people what they want to hear, but Waiyaki is prepared not merely to listen to the voice of the people, but to submit to the decisions it expresses. Even when he feels constantly under surveillance and constrained in his choice of action, he is able to contain his resentment and, via thoughts of his father, re-dedicate himself to serving the tribe. Waiyaki's rhetorical and ideological stance, and his concept of a leader as a servant of the people, is markedly different from Kabonyi's demagogic style and his more obvious intention to manipulate and ultimately control both audience and community. At the same time, the tension between Waiyaki's desire for greater freedom in the way he lives his life and his knowledge of the need for him to work on behalf of his people inaugurates one of Ngugi's enduring themes: the often fraught relationship between, and relative prioritising of, the individual and the collective (the latter construed as the community or the nation). His mother, in the quote above, articulates the typical or traditional view of this relationship, and it is one which – surprisingly in view of what we have seen – Waiyaki in the end is prepared to disregard.

Waiyaki's love for Nyambura (though it might appear oddly anæmic to provoke the taking up of such a firm stance by someone who previously found such action all too difficult) instantiates various kinds of reconciliation. At the level of the structure or form of the narrative, it brings together the public plot and the personal sub-plot; at the level of the divided community, it (potentially) effects a reunification of various groups, beliefs, etc. However, if it unites the public and personal, the individual and collective at the structural level, it represents a moment of catastrophic prioritising of one over the other: called upon to renounce Nyambura and reaffirm his oath of loyalty to the community and its concept of tribal purity, Waiyaki chooses his emotional commitment to one individual over his social and moral commitment to the collective, leading to his immediate denunciation by the people and loss of position and power. Although he has recently come to see Nyambura as a necessary element in the struggle for unity, his decision to choose her, while it may carry emotional power, has negative implications for both couple and community – though not everyone would see it that way. For some critics, this emergent Western-style individualism in Waiyaki is both positive and the key to the text. Werner Glinga, for example, argues that: 'The River Between is not a novel of leadership or education, but of a protagonist who wants to lead his life against the tide of his time.'[29] The latter is such a repetitive trope in the European novel of the last one hundred and fifty years that it inevitably raises the question of whether Glinga is simply reading Ngugi through a typical Western framework of novelistic expectations, or whether in fact Ngugi has produced something rather closer to the traditional European novel than it might at first appear.

Waiyaki, as we have seen, embodies a selection of the contradictions involved in the position of leadership. This is far from being an abstract issue, however, and in the post-colonial context in which Ngugi began publishing his novels, the idea of communal or national leadership was inseparable from the figure of Kenyatta, and the accompanying ideological and rhetorical inflation. As such, the prominence given to the question of leadership in *The River Between* cannot be ideologically neutral, and indeed a critic like David Maughan Brown would regard Ngugi as trapped by the dominant pro-Kenyatta ideology. It is, however, worth repeating (if in fact such repetition is needed after all that we have seen in the course of this chapter) that Waiyaki is hardly the rose-tinted or hagiographical portrait of the leader as saviour of the community which might reasonably have been expected from a writer in the grip of this particular dominant 'leaderist' ideology.

Similar kinds of contradictions persist in relation to the question of reconciliation. On one level, there is no obvious reason why reconciliation of opposing groups, divided commun-ities or antagonistic individuals should in any way be a bad thing – quite the opposite, in many people's opinion. At the same time, Kenyatta's post-independence rhetoric of national, even imperial, reconciliation (and historical amnesia) involved the ignoring of so much suffering and injustice, past and present, that it immediately became a loaded concept. Also, as Maughan Brown argues, in the literary context reconciliation is marked by Western aesthetic ideologies of balance, fairness, etc., which are deeply suspect, if not demonstrably retrograde.[30] Clearly, *The River Between* is a novel which is better at identifying or instantiating contradictions than it is at providing resolutions for them.

Weep Not, Child

If the historical distance and geographical isolation of *The River Between* seemed to provide Ngugi with the freedom to lessen that novel's specificity somewhat, that is scarcely an option with his next book *Weep Not, Child*, which is set in the 1940s and 50s, in the period covering the emergence of the armed phase of anti-colonial resistance in Kenya. There are parallels with the other novel, in that the story also details the rise and fall – though less extreme – of an educated young man, Njoroge (though he is far more of a peripheral figure in terms of the relations and distribution of power in his society than Waiyaki), as well as another star-crossed relationship which brings boy and girl together from opposing sides of the divided black community. The novel stands as part of the growing number of African depictions of childhood and maturation, such as Camara Laye's *The African Child*, or Tsitsi Dangarembga's *Nervous Conditions*, but it is also a (partial) account of the troubled Mau Mau period seen through the eyes of a young Gikuyu boy. Although the Mau Mau dimension makes *Weep Not, Child* much less of a simple narrative than *The African Child*, it is nevertheless related in a simple manner, as a linear narrative with a somewhat inconclusive ending.

One of the major differences from *The River Between* is the nature of British colonial power: its intrusiveness; its repressive and brutal deployment. In the intervening generation it has installed itself very much more thoroughly in Gikuyu territory, most conspicuously in terms of its hold over the land. Although Berman and Lonsdale have argued that British colonialism was by no means a homogenous entity, that there were, for instance, tensions between settlers and administrators, that different attitudes and agendas existed, there is nevertheless the feeling in *Weep Not Child*, that all aspects of the British presence – what Althusser would call the RSAs (repressive state apparatuses: the army and the police), the ISAs (ideological state apparatuses: education, religion, the bureaucracy), and civil society (the settlers in particular) – combine in a tightly knit distribution of power.[31] In particular, in the world of Njoroge and his family, British colonialism wears literally a single face, that of Howlands as farmer, employer, usurper of their ancestral lands, District Officer, torturer, etc. British power now operates more openly and extensively through its indigenous intermediaries or collaborators, especially those like Jacobo whom it has appointed as chiefs, those who in their desire to emulate and win approval from the colonialists become worse than them: 'The name of the Chief was becoming a terror in the land' (91). The repressive use of Jacobo appears as a deliberate strategy of Howlands':

> Howlands felt a certain gratifying pleasure. The machine
> he had set in motion was working. The blacks were destroy-
> ing the blacks. They would destroy themselves to the end.
> What did it matter with him if the blacks in the forest
> destroyed a whole village? (97)

While this makes very clear the deliberate, callous destruct-
iveness of British policy, it also indicates what can be seen as a
limitation of Ngugi's approach. Although on one level the
reduction of British colonial oppression to the figure of
Howlands may be justifiable in terms of the limited experience
and understanding of Njoroge, the idea that divisive tactics were
entirely his invention turns a systematic colonial policy into a
question of individual malice. It is all too easy for the reader to
lose sight of the British colonial apparatus behind Howlands:
apart from Jacobo and his few homeguards (and a walk-on part
for the other British interrogator), he seems to operate alone,
and this in turn creates an oddly skewed sense of the colonial
situation. Although there are references to the original British
theft of the land from the Gikuyu, it is almost as if Howlands
retains control of the land through sheer force of will and his
utterly obsessive desire to hold and master it. While the use of
an individual as the embodiment of a cause or representative of
a group might work with Waiyaki or Kabonyi (since that in a
sense is what they literally are), in general the reduction of the
systemic to the personal is fraught with problems.

   Occupation and retention of Gikuyu land represents one
kind of demonstration of white power; at the same time, its
possession is also a fundamental source of power within the
Gikuyu community (regardless of questions of basic survival or
the production and sale of surplus):

> If a man had plenty of money, many motor cars, but no
> land, he could never be counted as rich. A man who went
> with tattered clothes but had at least an acre of red earth
> was better off than the man with money. (19)

In such a context, loss of land is both cause and effect of lack of
power in the community, and it is unsurprising that Njoroge,

whose youth allows him to raise the naive but pertinent
questions, asks 'where did the land go?' The text supplies
different answers. Njoroge's father Ngotho gives his in terms
familiar from *The River Between*: Mugo wa Kibiro's prophecy –
ignored by his people – of the coming of the white men; their
gradual encroachment on the land; and the final expropriation
which occurred after the First World War. The knowledge –
previously withheld, or at least not made clear – that his family
are mere tenants of a white farmer on their own ancestral lands
prompts an angry response from Njoroge's half-brother Boro, a
question about the power and resolve of earlier generations
which echoes in several of Ngugi's novels: 'How could these
people have let the white man occupy the land without acting?
And what was all this superstitious belief in a prophecy' (27).
Action is what Boro resolves upon, and carries out as leader of a
Mau Mau unit; belief in prophecy is what keeps Ngotho on this
piece of land, waiting for the time when it will revert to its
rightful owners. The unspoken power struggle between Ngotho's
dogged determination to see out white usurpation of his land
and Howlands' violent obsession with holding on to 'his god',
mirrors (and again individualises) the larger struggle to prise
loose the grip of British colonial power on Kenya. The fact that
Ngotho loses (he is moved off the land and dismissed from his
job after attacking Jacobo) does not necessarily presage Mau
Mau defeat, but it certainly represents a great loss for Ngotho:
'… and yet he felt the loss of the land even more keenly than
Boro, for to him it was a spiritual loss. When a man was severed
from the land of his ancestors, where would he sacrifice to the
Creator?' (74). The importance of the land for the Gikuyu is
explained by Kenyatta:

> In studying the Gikuyu tribal organisation, it is necessary
> to take into consideration land tenure as the most
> important factor in the social, political, religious and
> economic life of the tribe. As agriculturalists, the Gikuyu
> people depend entirely on the land. It supplies them with
> the material needs of life, through which spiritual and
> mental contentment is achieved. Communion with the

ancestral spirits is perpetuated through contact with the soil in which the ancestors of the tribe lie buried. The Gikuyu consider the earth as the 'mother' of the tribe ... it is the soil that feeds the child through lifetime; and again after death it is the soil that nurses the spirits of the dead for eternity. Thus the earth is the most sacred thing above all that dwell in or on it. Among the Gikuyu the soil is especially honoured and an everlasting oath is to swear by the earth.[32]

Similarly, Ngugi emphasises the spiritual dimension, repeating as in *The River Between* the Gikuyu myth of the covenanting of the land by God to Gikuyu and Mumbi, the Adam and Eve-like parents of the people. Ironically, it is the unbeliever Howlands who, in his fixated and exorbitant manner of regarding the land as 'his god', reveals his 'unnatural' attitude towards it, in contrast to Ngotho.

In relation to ideas of community, *Weep Not Child* explores the contradictions of division and unity, unhealthy proximity and unhappy isolation, as well as solidarity and solitariness at all levels from the individual to the social. The *de facto* existence of something like a multi-racial society is acknowledged, but scarcely celebrated: the book opens with images of the strangeness and incomprehensibility of white men, and, in the monitory tale of the ugly, fly-ridden children born to African women and Italian prisoners of war, a strong image of the inadvisability of sex as inter-racial bonding. Indians are no better regarded than whites: 'You could never like the Indians because their customs were strange and funny in a bad way' (7). Though this (presumably childish) piece of xenophobia goes unsupported in the text, it is not rebutted in any way. In the face of funny and inscrutable foreigners, unidentified voices from the community say that 'black people should stick together' (8). Unfortunately, this kind of black solidarity proves impossible to achieve in any general or lasting way, and, paradoxically, white men can come to seem not too bad after all. Njoroge asks his brother:

'But why does he treat you like that? He is a black man.'
'Blackness is not all that makes a man,' Kamau said

bitterly. 'There are some people, be they black or white, who do not want others to rise above them … Some Europeans are better than Africans … That's why you at times hear father say he would rather work for a white man. A white man is a white man. But a black man trying to be a white man is bad and harsh.' (21)

Despite the fact that the object of this conversation, Kamau's employer Nganga, later demonstrates remarkable and unlooked for solidarity towards Njoroge and Kamau's family, the image of black traitors, and of blacks as behaving worse than whites towards their own people (even though the latter's origins lie in repetitious and self-serving assertions made by Europeans about the nature of the people they colonised) remains important in the book. For Ngotho during the brief moment of the strike, Jacobo symbolises this division and betrayal of black by black, and, completely uncharacteristically, he attacks him. Although Ngotho has reason to dislike Jacobo as his landlord, he now, in another version of the representative individualising of collect-ive struggles, sees them as standing for two opposed peoples: himself as champion of the blacks; Jacobo as champion of the whites. To some characters, the existence of people such as Jacobo means that the black community will always be divided: 'It would have been alright if it had been a white man, but a black man – like you and me! It shows that we black people will never be united. There must always be a traitor in our midst' (60). Among the points to note about this are, firstly, that it makes betrayal almost an inescapable existential fact for black people, rather than the historical result of the presence of colonialism and the divisive effect of its unequally distributed rewards and privileges. Secondly, not unlike the 'black people treat their own worse than whites do' attitude, it places the blame on black people. Thirdly, it ignores the fact that the grounds for considering someone a traitor may be dangerously mutable: in the brief mythic résumé of the story of Waiyaki in chapter 2, it is the unnamed Waiyaki who is killed, presumably as a traitor, and precisely for advocating community solidarity. Failure may be almost as divisive as betrayal: the perceived failure of Ngotho and his generation to do anything about the theft of the land in the past; his failure to take an appropriate stand now; his failure to prevent the arrest of Njeri and Kori; his failure to tell his family the full facts about their ancestral land – all these set son against father.

Earlier failure to resist the British is offset by the development of Gikuyu resistance as the novel progresses: the vague but recognisable reference to the 1922 march to protest against the arrest of the unnamed Harry Thuku; the strike; the emerging consciousness in Ngotho and others like him of the need to do something more than sit and wait for the land to be given back; the growth of support for Mau Mau; the taking of decisive action against the oppressors and the killing of Howlands and Jacobo. This might all seem very positive; however, David Maughan Brown is highly sceptical of Ngugi's representation of Mau Mau. For Maughan Brown, Ngugi is still too much under the influence of powerful aesthetic and ideological conventions, including ideas of Mau Mau brutality, irrationality, and animality, as well as the need for 'balance' in representation: 'The familiar "balance" formula, structurally requiring atrocities to be committed by guerrillas to legitimate the presence and actions of "security forces", is by and large content to take its cautionary narratives from the same "security forces" or from settlers.'[33] The 'cautionary narratives', drawing heavily on racist stereotyping and propagandist scaremongering, include: vicious Mau Mau brutality (they chop their victims into pieces with pangas); irrational violence and cruelty (they fight and kill for the sake of it); lack of solidarity or concern for other black people (they force the closure of schools, regardless of the effect on the pupils). In addition, sentences such as 'although there had been several deportations from villages and a few deaths, this was the first big direct blow by either Mau Mau or Serikali [the government] to the village community' (86) make the positions appear equivalent, as if, in this instance, both sides have an equal interest in attacking the village. Also, the results of resistance do not appear as particularly positive (not least for Njoroge's family). Ngotho dies after being tortured; Boro will be hanged;

Kamau is in prison; the killing of Jacobo strains the relationship between Njoroge and Mwihaki; Mau Mau activity seems to divide rather than unite the community. Part of the reason for the way in which Mau Mau is represented lies no doubt in Ngugi's choice of the immature and ill-informed Njoroge as focaliser, and Mwihaki's childish perceptions of the alienness and brutality of Mau Mau reinforce this, but even so, many of the questionable elements exist as narrative 'facts' rather than Njoroge's view of things.

One thing which Mwihaki and Njoroge share, apart from problematic perceptions of Mau Mau (and to which these perceptions may not be entirely unrelated) is the experience of education. While education is less of a crusade than it was in *The River Between*, it is given more prominence in the novel, as we follow Njoroge through his career from primary school to the prestigious Siriana High School. Education is also generally regarded more positively (or at least with less suspicion) than in the earlier novel, while an assertion such as 'Somehow the Gikuyu people always saw their deliverance as embodied in education' (104–5) shifts the 'messianic' burden from one individual to the education system. At the same time, this is indicative of a general over-estimating of the potential of education. The narrative voice, for example, tells us: 'In spite of the troubled time, people still retained a genuine interest in education. Whatever their differences, interest in knowledge and book learning was the one meeting point between people such as Boro, Jacobo and Ngotho' (104). The text, however, gives us no actual indication of any such meeting of minds, or indeed any significant interest in education on the part of the individuals mentioned. A different kind of over-estimation of education comes from the text itself: after all the examples of racial mistrust, dislike and separation mentioned earlier, it is interesting that the novel's one image of achieved community – multi-ethnic, multi-racial, multi-faith, harmonious, and (almost) non-hierarchical – is the elite school of Siriana: 'Njoroge at times wished the whole country was like this. This seemed a little paradise, a paradise where children from all walks of life and of different religious faiths could work together without any consciousness' (115). While it may be unintentional, the final phrase is revelatory: it is indeed only at the expense of being wilfully unconscious of the reality of the situation in Kenya that the harmony of such a paradisal state can be maintained.

Someone who does not over-estimate education is Ngotho: '"Education is everything," Ngotho said. Yet he doubted this because he knew deep inside his heart that land was everything. Education was good only because it would lead to the recovery of the lost lands' (39). Ngotho's view may be more pragmatic, but in keeping this to himself and paying lip service to received notions, he helps fuel Njoroge's serious and enduring over-estimation:

> He knew that for him education would be the fulfilment of a wider and more significant vision − a vision that embraced the demand made on him, not only by his father, but also by his mother, his brothers and even the village. He saw himself destined for something big, and this made his heart glow. (39)

In fact, the 'something big' turns out to be messianic: 'When these moments caught him, he actually saw himself as a possible saviour for the whole of God's country. Just let him get learning' (82). Without even a Chege-style prophecy to support this, Njoroge's imaginings seem preposterous. Such childishly-inflated imaginings are counterposed to the nationally-inflated hopes of the people, centred on the (apparently) prophesied 'Black Moses' of Jomo Kenyatta. *Weep Not, Child* was written at a time when Kenyatta's popularity was at its peak, before the limitations of his position and policies became painfully obvious, and when he appeared to many, particularly the ordinary people, as the man who embodied their deliverance from British colonialism. As such, Maughan Brown's criticism of what he sees as the greatly inflated way in which Kenyatta is represented in the novel may itself be something of an exaggeration: 'Where the "leadership" ideology is concerned, Ngugi uses his characters in *Weep Not, Child* to project the Kenyatta myth with a fervency which rivals that of *Suffering Without Bitterness* [Kenyatta's biography].'[34] Split between the delusions of leadership of Njoroge and the apparently failed leadership of the jailed Kenyatta, the novel has no alternative figure to propose (and certainly not the directionless, amoral, guerrilla leadership of Boro), and perhaps its inability or refusal to imagine a replacement could be perceived as an endorsement of the power of 'the Kenyatta myth' at this historical moment.

Historically, Kenyatta was the figure identified with ideas of community or national leadership, but the image is one which recurs in Ngugi's work, for instance in his play *The Black Hermit*, written and performed in this period though not published for several years. It is set in the post-colonial present, and centres on a young man, Remi, with similar ideas and a similar (if anything rather heavier) burden of communal expectation to Waiyaki and Njoroge. *Black Hermit*, while it retains religious overtones, is not as promising in salvational terms as *Black Moses* or *Black Messiah* – rightly, as it turns out. Reluctantly persuaded to return from a very 'modern' life in the city, Remi hopes to overcome the retrograde effects of tribalism and Christianity in his community, and, like Waiyaki, to unite his people. Throwing himself into the task, berating everyone for their backwardness, he declares 'everything will give way to my leadership', insisting 'I now know all. My stay in the city has taught me everything.'[35] As in *The River Between*, the public task is complicated by emotions, the 'public' narrative overtaken by the personal, the modernising drive undone by archaic attitudes, and the dream of communal unity unfulfilled. Before fleeing to the city, Remi had, according to tribal custom, married his brother's widow, whom he had secretly loved but whom he (wrongly) assumed did not love him. On his return, she (wrongly) assumes that he does not love her, and kills herself. His mother's caustic assessment: 'education and big learning has taught him nothing', seems very accurate at this level.[36]

The complicating effect of gender roles and relations returns us to *Weep Not, Child*. Here, early in the novel, gender relations are foregrounded in the shape of the problematic or unprofitable nature of inter-racial sex – the former in the case mentioned earlier of African women who slept with Italian prisoners of war and whose children were all ugly and diseased; the latter in the context of the conversation in the barber's shop. Of the former we are told: 'Some people said that this was a punishment. Black people should not sleep with white men who ruled them and treated them badly' (6). Leaving aside the point that the black 'people' are precisely *not* sleeping with their white rulers, no such comment is passed on the African men who sleep with white women during the war. Here again, the problem is seen to lie with the women since they prostitute themselves, their lack of moral substance matched by their physical shortcomings. Although the barber, in answer to the question 'how are they …?' about white women, replies 'Not different. Not different', which might suggest some common humanity, he continues 'I like a good fleshy black body with sweat. But they are … you know … so thin … without flesh … nothing' (9). While the ability to 'buy' a white woman might look like localised access to (gendered) power of a sort for a black man, it is ultimately unprofitable because you don't get much for your money. The reduction of white women to 'nothing' is part of that process – the most obvious example being returned black ex-servicemen – where increased knowledge of the colonial rulers relativises their power – or at least their ideological or hegemonic power, if it does not immediately alter their coercive power to rule. Nevertheless, loosening the hegemonic hold is an important step towards people being able to loosen the more material forms of power and control.

The barber shop conversation passes into Ngotho's thoughts about his own women, his wives Njeri and Nyokabi, and the complacent sexism of an untroubled patriarch:

> But you could not quite trust women. They were fickle and very jealous. When a woman was angry no amount of beating would pacify her. Ngotho did not beat his wives much. On the contrary, his home was well known for being a place of peace. All the same, one had to be careful. (11)

Subsequent events, however, while they do not alter the loyalty of Ngotho's wives towards him, constitute a profound crisis of his patriarchal role and his masculine identity. He joins the strike, insisting on being a man in his own house (and despite the accurate prediction of its failure by Nyokabi). Not only does the strike fail, it fails because of Ngotho's attack on Jacobo, and he thus loses face with, and influence over, his son Boro. Despite this diminishment, Ngotho refuses the further loss of patriarchal power which would result from being told by Boro to take the Mau Mau oath. The decline continues when he is able to do nothing to prevent the arrest of Kori and Njeri: 'It was too late. He came back to his seat, a defeated man, a man who cursed himself for being a man with a lost manhood' (80). His later, literal castration at the hands of Howlands seems an almost incidental confirmation of what has already happened to him.

The relation of Ngotho and Boro raises the recurrent issue of generational (male) authority, as well as the more precisely historicised question of the extent to which in the circumstances of mid twentieth-century Kenya – social disruption, family dispersal, the move to the cities, not to mention the anti-colonial struggle – fathers can retain traditional forms of obedience from children. There is a sense in which if knowledge of the outside world can result in a relativising of the colonialists' power it can have a similar effect on patriarchal control. Although Boro would seem to have imposed a more secular or modern relationship, where a father would have to earn his son's respect and obedience rather than simply demand it, he nevertheless returns at the end to beg forgiveness of his dying father in a manner which is entirely traditional. It is also noteworthy that Njoroge who, like Waiyaki, has undergone the most extensive exposure to the 'modernising' effect of education, does nothing to disobey or lessen the authority of his father (though each of course has a relationship with the daughter of the enemy).

Some similar aspects of patriarchy and masculinity are visible in Howlands, though figured much more brutally and uncompromisingly. Like Ngotho, Howlands refuses to listen or submit to his wife: 'He would not give in to either Mau Mau or his wife. He would reduce everything to his will' (77–8). His final words are an expression of gendered colonial power: '"This is my land." Mr Howlands said this as a man would say, "This is my woman"' (129). As his real wife loses importance, the farm shifts from being his god to being his wife: 'For the farm was the woman whom he had wooed and conquered. He had to keep an eye on her lest she should be possessed by someone else' (127).

The relationship between Njoroge and Mwihaki is longer-lasting than that between Waiyaki and Nyambura, but does not particularly open out into discussion of gender roles. Nevertheless, we see Mwihaki move from an early position of superiority *vis-à-vis* Njoroge (she is a class ahead of him at school and he does not like it), via being comforted by his empty rhetoric (as the situation in the country worsens, she likes him to promise brighter futures – as if he could deliver), to a desire for him to take control – at their final meeting she cries: 'You must save *me*, please Njoroge' (133). Significantly, when Njoroge cannot take up the offered (masculine) role of saviour, an important reversal takes place. Firstly, Mwihaki reasserts her own individuality – though crucially this consists of an awareness of responsibility to others and a refusal to be distracted from it by the selfish individualism of Njoroge's plan for the two of them to run away together. From being in a position where 'she wanted to sink into his arms and feel a man's strength around her weak body' (133), she emerges stronger, and it is Njoroge who proves weak, lapsing into self-pity which would have been fatal had he had the strength to go through with his suicide attempt.

Emergent class formations are among the things which divide Mwihaki and Njoroge, and class – appropriately enough, in view of the historical differences – is a more important feature of *Weep Not, Child* than it was of *The River Between*. While Gikuyu society, like any other, was obviously stratified by wealth – and indeed evolved a complex sense of, in Berman and Lonsdale's phrase, 'civic virtue' around questions of wealth and poverty – it is colonialism and its capitalist social relations which introduce Western-style class formation, and in the Kenyan context this is ultimately related to the ownership or not of land. One aspect of class formation was the deliberate creation by the British of a class which would eventually develop into a black bourgeoisie as class stratification and social organisation progressed increasingly along Western or Western-defined lines. This was originally based on, but not confined to, unfairly allocated grants of land. In addition, it involved allowing exceptional production of cash crops (in Jacobo's case, it is pyrethrum daisies, which Njoroge has on occasion earned money picking). However, even in those rare instances when Kenyans were allowed to grow cash crops, they were not allowed to sell their produce for the same price as whites. The combination of land ownership and cash crop production created a huge disparity between favoured individuals and the bulk of the population, but it was not an absolute division. In the novel we see signs of a nascent petit bourgeoisie in the shape of individuals who own small businesses and small amounts of land. For the mass of the expropriated rural population, however, class formation means proletarianisation, and Kenya stands as one of the clearest examples of the (forcible) creation of a colonised proletariat where none had previously existed. The organisation of an adequate labour force to work on the land had historically been a problem in Gikuyu society, but not a major one; the importation of Western-size farms and Western-style farming made it a major problem, not least because it had hitherto not been organised on a cash basis. The British, however, required the mass, if not wholesale, entry of the Gikuyu into a cash economy; they also wanted a workforce which, in order to ensure its continued 'loyalty', could not survive by any means other than the sale of its labour to its colonial rulers. Land allocation to Gikuyu communities was therefore calculated at a level which would not permit adequate subsistence farming – which would 'divert' them from their proper function of wage labour for the British since they would no longer be dependent. One choice facing the Gikuyu and other groups in the mid century was whether to be part of the rural or the urban proletariat, and choices made along these lines contribute to the disintegration of Ngotho's family. Gikuyu ideologies of the virtue of wealth and self-improvement were elaborated in a more egalitarian society, and certainly one which did not actively militate against self-advancement in the way colonialist capitalism does for the majority of people. The failure, therefore, to achieve self-advancement is a particular loss of standing – which is one reason for the emphasis on the education of the younger generation, education providing one of the few obvious avenues for social mobility. It is perhaps no more than typical of Njoroge, and the bleak vision of *Weep Not, Child*, that he fails in this as in so much else.

Maughan Brown argues that class differences are largely gestural in *Weep Not, Child*, and while it is true that the text does not dwell on them, we could suggest that at one and the same time they constitute a partial ideological blind spot as well as being fundamental to what happens in the novel. Mwihaki thinks 'her world and Njoroge's world stood somewhere outside petty prejudices, hatreds and class differences'(88). Although Njoroge does not explicitly share these sentiments – and particularly not at this juncture – they represent a succinct formulation of the ideology of the transcendence of the political by the personal, especially as embodied in the couple, as we saw with Waiyaki and Nyambura. At the same time, it is awareness of how class is being constituted (i.e. especially in relation to the colonial system of domination and expropriation) which sets Kenyans against one another. Jacobo is crystallised as the enemy for Ngotho because of his betrayal in class and racial terms: the fact that as the richest man in the area he is counselling workers not to protest against conditions of injustice, and that he is also doing so on behalf of the British.

Ngugi's first two novels end in different kinds of disarray (personal, familial, communal) and narrative irresolution. The return to the beginning in *The River Between* with the image of the Honia flowing on does nothing to resolve the dilemmas facing the community it divides – though such a return inevitably suggests a relativising of human problems in the broader perspective of natural rhythms and flows (however problematic an ideology that may involve). Critics have argued that the lack of resolution in the narrative is the result of Ngugi's own inability to imagine a resolution, in part because of his own closeness to the events portrayed in *Weep Not, Child*, and also because of his over-identification with the male protagonists of the two novels. The possibility that Ngugi might actually *choose* to end in irresolution as representative of a) the community's lack of a clear solution in *The River Between*, and b) the absence of a historical solution to the problems of *Weep Not, Child*, is for some reason less attractive than notions of artistic failure or psychological blockage. There may be more to be said for the suggestion that Ngugi's own involvement with the colonially-imposed education system is part of the reason for the complex/ contradictory handling of various issues, including that of education, in these novels. If that were the case, though, one would expect this complexity to become more fraught as Ngugi himself moved through the system, and on to university abroad, but as *A Grain of Wheat* shows, this is not in fact the case.

A Grain of Wheat

A Grain of Wheat completes what we could regard as the first cycle of Ngugi's novels covering the period up to the moment of Kenyan independence in 1963, all written in the 1960s, all written under the name James Ngugi, and all marked by a broadly liberal/humanist outlook. Having said that, we might expect *A Grain of Wheat* to be essentially similar to the earlier two novels, but while there are indeed a number of continuities and similarities in theme and content, the novel marks a significant shift, especially at the level of form. It tells the story of the Gikuyu village of Thabai in the week leading up to independence, but does so through a much more sophisticated use of narrative form and time than might have been expected from the author of *Weep Not, Child* or *The River Between*. The novel combines a four-day time span in the present with flashbacks covering a number of years, and the interweaving of chronologies and narratives of different characters builds towards the final moments. This process involves an accumulation of insight and understanding by both characters and readers as the truth of events becomes known and motivations become clearer. This greater structural complexity is matched at the level of character. Ngugi uses a greater number and variety of characters than in previous novels. There is also the achievement of greater psychological complexity, not least through the use of adults rather than adolescents as focalisers, and this increased complexity extends to the representation of the British: there is, for example, a more extensive treatment of John Thompson than of Howlands in *Weep Not, Child*, and an attempt through him to embody some of the ideological contradictions of colonialism. This kind of effort to present both sides in conflict, though without suggesting that their positions or their validity are in any way equivalent, might bear superficial similarities to the ideology of 'balance' of which Maughan Brown was so suspicious, but has more in common with Bakhtin's dialogical novel. (In addition, the use of a range of focalisers might argue for *A Grain of Wheat* as in fact a kind of transitional text between the dialogic and a more properly polyphonic novel such as *Petals of Blood*.)

The gradual construction of communal narrative from the interwoven stories of a range of individuals from the village, combining present time and flashback, has seemed to many critics to mark an impressive advance – but not to all:

> But in spite of the apparent formlessness and lack of narrative distance, in spite of a forest of static and undeveloped characters that are methodically eliminated immediately after being introduced, in spite of too many confusing flashbacks, and in spite of the improbable social awareness given to illiterate peasant characters who seem to have had no formal education but can quote from the Bible and know all the current world events, one cannot lose sight of the fact that an unbroken though thin thread runs throughout the novel.[37]

Praise indeed. The irony is that this kind of dismissal of the developing complexity of an African novelistic technique comes from an African critical perspective which is strongly identified with Western canonical literature and dominant aesthetic ideologies, and which at other times would tend to be patronising, if not dismissive, towards African writers precisely for their perceived inability to compete with the complex literary products of Western culture. The good thing is that such attitudes are rarer than they once were, though as we shall see in the next chapter on *Petals of Blood*, Ngugi can still rouse critics to passionate denunciations of his work.

With its focus on the (supposedly) climactic moment of the achievement of national independence in December 1963, *A Grain of Wheat* is the most precisely located of Ngugi's novels; it also demonstrates a much greater awareness of historical process and the ways in which individual histories both intersect with, and form constitutive elements in, communal histories, and while it is not – and is not meant to be – a simple cross-section of the nation, it does nevertheless possess an important representative breadth. Rather than the easily available triumphalist version of independence from the point of view of the national leadership, the reader is presented with a narrative 'history from below' – a view of what national independence means to ordinary people, both in terms of how they understand it, and what it implies for their future. In this, Ngugi demonstrates his loyalty to the perspective of the majority at a time when the narrative of heroic leadership would assert its greatest ideological influence and attraction.

Having said that, it still needs to be pointed out that leadership is one of the themes carried over from the earlier novels, along with others such as education and the land, which are treated in varying degrees of depth and detail. The question of the land, for instance, is both less foregrounded in the text and ultimately more of a problem to the community. For once, briefly, we see someone working the land (in general, a curious narrative absence, given the importance of the subject) but it is Mugo, and his work is spasmodic and unproductive. Perhaps because people are anticipating the return of the stolen land after independence it is not discussed as an important issue, but it crops up in a particularly disturbing way: a new kind of large-scale land theft, but this time perpetrated by their own black MP.

Education is seen to have diminished in importance in the novel even more than the land. School becomes the occasion for Kihika, the future Mau Mau leader and martyr partly modelled on the historical figure of Dedan Kimathi, to mark a decisive break with Western-style education revealed as factually inaccurate, culturally denigratory, and personally repressive. It is significant, nevertheless, that his resistance occurs over the interpretation of the Bible, and the fact that the latter remains both the ethical touchstone and political guide for the leader of the resistance struggle has important implications for the ideological stance of the novel. For none of the other major characters in the novel does formal education occupy a position even remotely resembling its importance for Waiyaki and Njoroge, and it is left to Kihika's shadowy younger brother Kariuki to perform the obligatory, if here perfunctory, role of the only boy from his region to go to Siriana.

As with the other two themes, leadership has arguably lost some of its earlier prominence, but has become more complex and ironic. The novel offers two fictional leader figures (as false and true messiahs, in so far as it continues to operate in a salvational mode) in Mugo and Kihika, and behind them the increasingly problematic figure of the real leader, Kenyatta. In its account of various leaders, the second chapter gives a history of the development of 'the Movement', prefigured in the historical Waiyaki, embodied in Harry Thuku, and reaching its apogee in Kenyatta; it also weaves in the fictional Kihika, and an account of his triumph (the capture of the garrison at Mahee), betrayal, torture, and execution. In one sense, what Waiyaki, Harry Thuku and Kihika share as leaders is their failure at a personal level (despite which, 'the Movement' continued to grow); and while at the moment of the book's production – and even more at the moment of the events of the narrative – Kenyatta could still be thought of as the one who would redeem the whole lineage of failed leaders, their history and their examples make it more likely that he too will fail. Even in the present of the narrative, however, the prospect of the loss of the past as a cultural and political resource, epitomised in the reduction of Gikuyu and Kenyan history to nothing more than a succession of failed leaders, is one of the most difficult things for the detainees in the prison camp to contemplate: 'He [Harry Thuku] had come back a broken man, who promised eternal co-operation with his oppressors, denouncing the Party he had helped to build. What happened yesterday could happen today. The same thing, over and over again, throughout history' (106). At another level, of course, the glorious resistance and martyr-dom embodied in the likes of Waiyaki and Kihika are anything but failure. Although Kenyatta is praised ('Jomo had lost the case at Kapenguria. The white man would silence the father and the orphans would be left without a helper' (105)), Kihika is the leader who counts in the novel: the celebrations planned to mark *Uhuru* (independence) in the village are as much to do with Kihika – enshrining his memory; unmasking his betrayer – as with national independence. Kihika is also, for better or worse, the leader most associated with the Christian elements, above all the messianic, which pervade the book. Although at first he merely thinks of himself as a saint and leader, along Gandhian lines, he later talks, and is talked about, in explicitly Christ-like terms: General R, for example, refers to 'Kihika's crucifixion' (26), and after his death 'a combined body of Homeguards and Police whipped and drove people from Thabai and other ridges to see the body of the rebel dangling on the tree' (17).

Kihika's use of Biblical imagery and phraseology and the fact that verses from Exodus, St John's Gospel, and Revelations (underlined in red or black from Kihika's personal Bible we are told) serve as epigrams for the different sections of the novel, have seemed excessive to some, or more usually, an unresolved effect of Ngugi's own earlier immersion in Christianity. The possibility that such a deployment of Biblical imagery might be an appropriate strategy for the Gikuyu in the 1950s tends not to be considered. Berman and Lonsdale suggest, however, that:

> They [educated Gikuyu] then used the Bible as a library of instructive stories of united national struggle behind inspired leadership. Tales of civic virtue now echoed Exodus as well as *ituika* [the ritualised transfer of power from one generation to another].[38]

Whether or not Christian imagery constituted the best available discourse of anti-colonial resistance is another question.

The aura of personalised messianism surrounding Kihika is mitigated, however, by his conviction that anyone prepared to sacrifice themselves for the greater good of national liberation is Christ-like: 'I die for you, you die for me, we become a sacrifice for one another. So I can say that you, Karanja, are Christ. I am Christ. Everybody who takes the Oath of Unity to change things in Kenya is a Christ' (95). The messianism is also diminished by being shared by Mugo, even though his vision of himself as a man with a mission and someone who would 'lead his people across the desert to the new Jerusalem' (134), seems to belong to that same realm of ungrounded messianism as Njoroge's. The somewhat complicated question remains, however, whether all that separates Kihika's version from Mugo and Waiyaki's is the fact that he is prepared to act on the conviction and act ethically, since there is no *a priori* reason why his initial vision should be any more credible than the others', and hence whether this confirms Kihika's later democratic messianism or whether it ends up dangerously confirming the fantasies of Mugo and Njoroge and problematising the whole notion of inspired leadership, or even leadership *tout court*. The novel can be read as a dramatic embodiment of this problem, as throughout the week of its 'real' present narrative time, the villagers press Mugo to become their leader, and he struggles to weigh the competing claims of his lifelong desire to be left alone, his guilt and recognition of his unfitness for leadership because of his betrayal of Kihika to the British, and his dream of power as belated compensation for the life he has led. Certainly, the near miss which Mugo represents for Thabai, the fact that the combination of individual desire and collective encouragement almost results in his becoming their leader and is prevented only by his unexpected last-minute confession, is intended as a warning. As Ngugi says in *Detained*: 'I tried through Mugo, who carried the burden of mistaken revolutionary heroism, to hint at the possibilities of the new Kenyatta.'[39] The 'new' Kenyatta is one who confirms the real failure of Kenyan leaders – that of recanting earlier radical positions and finding an accommodation with colonialist policies – and his great predecessor here is Harry Thuku in the 1930s. Whether or not Mugo is intended as a coded representation of the dangers of Kenyatta's shift, he clearly shows the problem of mistaken historical information, of the construction of popular myths, and of the scope for unscrupulous demagoguery. The novel contrasts at a distance, but does not directly comment on, the situation of Mugo – the 'betrayer' who almost becomes a leader but is prevented by his new-found honesty – with that of the local MP – the 'leader' who has already begun the betrayal of his people, stealing their land with a complete lack of honesty or scruples.

If Mugo represents one path to 'bad' leadership, via the misplaced trust of the people, Karanja represents another, via betrayal of the people in collaboration with the British, as he becomes homeguard and eventually chief. Such behaviour constitutes an irredeemable separation from the people, and his mother, in words which echo those of Waiyaki's mother in *The River Between*, tells him (rather belatedly, one feels) 'do not go against the people. A man who ignores the voice of his own people comes to no good end' (226). While this is the powerful received wisdom of the Gikuyu people, and while in the novel Karanja seems to be headed for 'no good end', collaboration, as Ngugi has bitterly commented on numerous occasions since, nevertheless proved a most useful route to post-colonial power and wealth for numbers of his countrymen.

The collaborationist behaviour of Karanja is, as critics have pointed out, just one of the forms which betrayal takes in the novel. Others include the betrayal of Kihika by Mugo, Gikonyo's betrayal in confessing the Mau Mau oath in order to secure his release from prison, and the 'betrayal' of Gikonyo by his wife Mumbi in sleeping with his long-time rival Karanja.

What is striking is the way in which betrayal of the collective (the community or some other group) is rationalised in terms of individual emotional needs or desires, and the way in which the latter are seen as more compelling. Thus, Mugo's betrayal of Kihika (and their people's cause) is ascribed to his feeling that Kihika has everything while he has nothing – the 'everything' being the positive personal relations which Mugo has never enjoyed. In a way which is more ideologically revelatory, both Gikonyo and Karanja commit acts of betrayal of the collective because each of them wants Mumbi. At the very least, this represents the same prioritising of personal over communal good which we saw in *The River Between*; in addition, it almost places the blame on Mumbi for the betrayals, making her, like the primal Eve figure whom, mythologically, her name evokes, the cause of man's fall from grace (rather than his own weakness). In contrast, her 'betrayal' of Gikonyo is ironically the result of her joy at hearing of his release from prison. The subliminal blaming of Mumbi is at odds with the way she is generally represented in the book: sensitive, caring, emotionally generous, a good wife (but with a mind and will of her own); the emotional, almost the moral centre of the novel. As such, she is the first fully developed example of the strong female characters who become increasingly important in Ngugi's work, and indicative of shifts in his depiction of gender issues. Although Elleke Boehmer suggests that Mumbi is 'consistently viewed only in [her] relation to men', it would be possible to turn this around and argue that the extent to which the central male characters achieve or experience significant existence is precisely in relation to her.[40] That obviously applies to the desire of Gikonyo and Karanja, their inability to live apart from her, the things they do because of her; it also applies to the awakening of Mugo to moral responsibility as a result of her effect on him.

The representation of women in the novel is certainly interpreted in radically divergent ways: for Judith Cochrane, the minor character Njeri 'reveals the great strength and deter-mination of Gikuyu woman in her impassioned vow to devote herself to Kihika', while for Elleke Boehmer she is just another example of the book's construction of woman as victim.[41] While there are problems with over-generalising, even essentialising, in a phrase such as 'the great strength ... of Gikuyu woman', there are also problems with seeing Njeri's courageous choice as mere victimhood, not least because she stands as a modern example of Kenyan women's involvement in anti-colonial resistance, in the tradition of earlier heroines such as Me Kitilili and Mary Kinyanjui, and as a fictional counterpart to Dedan Kimathi's companion Wanjiru. (Even though one might want to query the gender ideology in this image of female self-sacrifice for love of the male warrior hero, the ideology can also work the other way round, with Karanja and Gikonyo ready to sacrifice themselves for Mumbi.)

Even if women are not always victims, there is one area where they seem ideologically doomed to fail:

> In *A Grain of Wheat* the story is told of the woman Wangu Makeri, who ruled over a large area in Muruanga until she broke one of the tribal taboos by dancing naked in public. She is labelled by Ngugi as the last of the great Gikuyu women, yet in women like Muthoni, Mumbi and Nyambura, Ngugi has given us glimpses of the kind of charm, beauty and power once wielded by the female rulers of old.[42]

The problem with this, apart from the fact that Ngugi does not call Wangu the last of the great Gikuyu women, is that her importance lies in the fact that she figures as a historical example of a potent ideological mythic notion: female rule as misrule – whether despotic, as in the tale of the distant matriarchal past (a brief version of which also appears in *The River Between*) or, as in Wangu's case, excessive in its disorderly deployment of 'charm, beauty and [sexual] power'. The unmentioned facts that the historical Wangu was a British appointee, and that she danced the *kibaata*, reserved for male warriors, might cast a somewhat different light on the forms of her transgression. Nevertheless, the trope recurs throughout the novel, for example in Gatu's story of the Queen of England offering herself to him in exchange for his land, or the attitude of the men of Thabai, who 'finding women like Mumbi on the roof hammering in nails, stopped to tease them: it was all because a new Wangu – in England – had been crowned: what good ever came from a woman's rule?', accusing them also of sending 'all the men to detention, for their penises to rot there, unwilling husbands to Queen Elizabeth' (141). Charm and beauty some of Ngugi's female characters may have, but at this stage, real power is something they are not allowed to get their hands on – though they are felt to possess negative 'dark power', which Mugo feels Mumbi wields over him.

Women may not have real power, but the British do – for the time being, at least. British colonial power, though still strongly identified with individual figures such as District Officer Robson, and his successor John Thompson, is seen less to emanate from their personal characteristics than was the case with Howlands in *Weep Not, Child*, for instance. Instead, there is the full machinery of the repressive system: informers, home-guards, the enforced centralisation of the 'villagisation' scheme which turns communities into prison camps in all but name, the prison camps themselves, beatings and torture, killings ('judicial' – like Kihika's, and extra-judicial – the majority). At the same time, the psychology of the colonisers is important (as Ngugi's reading of Fanon during the writing of *A Grain of Wheat* would emphasise), and the brittle nature of John Thompson's liberal colonialism (construed as a more properly moral and cultural mission) is revealed. Ironically, in view of the anti-colonial nationalism which is at the heart of the novel, Thompson's vision is of the Empire as one (British) nation, 'based on the just proposition that all men were created equal' (54). Once the colonised begin to ask themselves whether they want to accept the gift of British culture, order or civilisation, and to answer in the negative, then Thompson's frustrated paternalism turns to fury. This is paralleled in his career as prison camp commandant at Rira, where his previously successful liberal regime runs aground on the resistance of the detainees – Mugo because he has nothing to tell; the others, who have, but won't tell – and he is reduced to brutality. It is significant that after his attempts at an enlightened, even philosophical approach to Africa (which is what his never written book *Prospero in Africa* was intended to be) his final assessment should be the hoary old (but reassuring) colonialist cliché: 'We are not beaten yet ... Africa cannot do without Europe' (166). On one level, the whites are indeed beaten: Kenya is independent, and the assertion of African incapacity is vacuous, self-serving and simply wrong. In the longer historical view, however, and in ways which Ngugi's subsequent novels address, Thompson is right: the West was anything but beaten, and, in conjunction with African politicians, refused to allow Africa to 'do without Europe'.

If John Thompson signifies colonial power's readiness to slip from the hegemonic mode (getting Africans to believe in British culture, and adopt it willingly) to the coercive mode (beating them when they are unwilling) the novel also shows that the hegemonic strategy can be successful, particularly in terms of its effects on individuals like Karanja. Somewhere between hegemony and coercion lies the complex and disturbing situation which General R experiences when he tries to defend his mother against his brutal father, but is attacked by her for his pains. Significantly, it is subsequent collective experience which enables understanding of the individual one: 'It was only later when he [General R] saw how so many Kenyans could proudly defend their slavery that he understood his mother's reaction' (212). Here the brutality of coercive domination (colonial or patriarchal) produces the active vocal consent which is supposed to be part of hegemony, but whether the pathology is collective or individual, it is no less easy to deal with.

In general, power in *A Grain of Wheat* operates, and is understood, in more diverse ways than in the earlier novels. It appears in more individualised forms, both as personal magnetism (the power of the otherwise unattractive Van Dyke over Margery Thompson) and as power wielded for personal rather than communal ends (Mugo desires, and Karanja obtains, power because of the attraction it holds of not having to account to anyone for its arbitrary despotic or lethal utilisation). It is noticeable that it is the two characters most alienated from the community who dream of this dehumanised use of it. For Karanja, it is simply the power to kill with no questions asked; in the case of Mugo, for whom power and greatness are synonymous, it takes the rather more formalised shape of the unquestionable power of the judge over life and death. In both instances, but particularly that of Karanja, it is power derived from collaboration, rather than, in the case of someone like Jacobo in *Weep Not, Child*, from their (newly acquired) class position. Karanja also sees power and power struggles in racialised terms: although his decision to stay in Thabai and work for the whites is explained in emotional terms (he wants above all to be near Mumbi), he is also portrayed as a fervent believer in 'whiteman's power', and the power which he parasitically derives from it: 'Had he himself not experienced that power, which also ruled over the souls of men, when he, as Chief, could make circumcised men cower before him, women scream by a lift of his finger?' (156). His vision of white power as permanence and progress also reflects a different but related form of alienation in its acceptance of white ideology: 'whiteman's power, unmovable as a rock, a power that had built the bomb and transformed a country from wild bush and forests into modern cities ... and all this in the space of sixty years' (156). The discovery that white power, especially in the shape of John Thompson who symbolises it for Karanja, is anything but 'unmovable' is a traumatic one, not least because Karanja is frightened of black power and its ability to move the colonial rock.

One source of black power – which Kihika realises is more powerful than the bomb – is the unity of the people, and this is one of the important lessons he draws from Gandhi. In *Weep Not, Child* the lack of unity among Kenyans, and in contrast, the unified force represented by the British, are seen as crucial in determining the outcome of the struggle. In *A Grain of Wheat* on the other hand, there is a sense of growing unity, represented among other things by 'the Movement', Mau Mau, and the belief in the success of the fight for independence. Among the symbols (and practices) of unity are the oaths administered by Mau Mau, which were more numerous and their use more widespread, than is suggested in the novel, where the (single) oath seems to be restricted to men fairly closely linked with Mau Mau. Maughan Brown, for example, suggests that ninety per cent of the adult Gikuyu population had taken the Oath of Unity, the first and most general of the oaths, which – unlike the *Batuni* or 'platoon' oath – did not include a commitment to kill for the cause if the situation demanded it. For both sides, a lot hinged on the keeping, or not, of the oaths: 'The detainees had agreed not to confess the oath or give any details about Mau Mau: how could anybody reveal the binding force of the Agikuyu in their call for African freedom?' (105). Despite this – and as a sign of the fragile nature of the actuality, if not the vision, of popular unity – confess is precisely what Gikonyo does, in order to allow him to return to Mumbi. Surprisingly, perhaps, given the declared importance of keeping the oath secret, there is no apparent moral censure attached to him for this action, either from the narrative voice or from characters such as General R and Lieutenant Koinandu. This can be read as a narrative agreement with the order of priorities Gikonyo personifies (yet again, the personal over the collective) or a more complex understanding of questions of guilt than some of the rhetoric of heroes and traitors would suggest.

> In his essay 'On Heroes and Uhuru Worship' Ali Mazrui suggests that 'perhaps part of the pervasive transform-ation of independence [is] that there should be a revision of a nation's martyrology'. The traditional pattern of immaculate hero and damned villain must be replaced by a process of 'selective memory' wherein the independent citizen attempts to know his past without condemning any of the countrymen with whom he must build a new nation. In *A Grain of Wheat* Ngugi extends Mazrui's analysis by demonstrating the need for a complete re-examination of traditional concepts of heroism, martyr-dom and villainy.[43]

If Monkman is correct here in his final assertion about what Ngugi is demonstrating (and it is not at all certain that Ngugi is doing anything so drastic or thoroughgoing), the question nevertheless remains whether he is extending Mazrui's analysis in a Mazrui-type direction. This is important, because the concepts of partial memory, reconciliation, and no condemnation, were key ones for Kenyatta, and ones which Ngugi will vigorously attack in later novels. The fact that it is Mugo who tells Gikonyo 'the government says we should bury the past' (67), suggests that it is not to be given too much weight as a guide for future conduct. Also, it is contrasted with the non-governmental desire of those like General R to preserve a full, not a partial memory (in this case, of Kihika, his betrayal and death) as well as to exact belated and appropriate justice (revolutionary, General R calls it) for the betrayals of the Mau Mau war. In particular, it is necessary to recognise the impact of deliberate forgetting in this context: firstly, because of the general and continuing cultural importance of historical memory for the Gikuyu (though obviously not only for them) as a basis for the organisation of collective identity and social and political decision making; secondly, deriving from this and operating in a more specific context, full historical memory, as we have seen, is a vital element in the empowering and mobilising process necessary for anti-colonial resistance.

The idea of 'rewriting the past' occurs in different forms: Kenyatta does it, as we have just seen; we might also regard Ngugi as doing it in the changes he made to *A Grain of Wheat*, the revised version being published in 1986 as part of the revamping of Heinemann's 'African Writers' series. Rewriting the past also has differing connotations. The negative kind, popularly associated with Stalinism, where facts are simply altered, truths denied and people expunged from the historical narrative, is precisely the sort of process in which Ngugi sees the Kenyatta regime engaged: constructing a version of the recent past based on denial, distortion and omission. A 'positive' form of rewriting would include the kind of project on which Ngugi himself is embarked, offering better representations of Africa in general, and Mau Mau in particular, than are provided by colonialist or neo-colonialist historiography. As well as questions of general orientation, this involves matters of historical detail. For instance, in the revisions to his novel, Ngugi alters the number of Kenyans killed by the British while protesting at the arrest of Harry Thuku from 15 to 150. This is not a case of wanting to make colonialism look as brutal as possible, but of incorporating more recent and reliable information – though the fact that it does highlight the brutality of colonialism is no doubt a bonus.

Another of Ngugi's changes to the novel might appear to have less to do with that kind of attention to historical detail. In the revised edition, 'the Party' becomes 'the Movement'. Carole Sicherman suggests that this reflects Ngugi's dissatisfaction with the accommodationist and reactionary behaviour of Kenyatta's KANU (Kenyan African National Union) party.[44] In addition to this negative reason, we might suggest that 'Movement' implies a much broader – and non-party – nature. This, as we will see in later chapters, is important to that aspect of Ngugi's revisionism which, in the face of denials by Western and Kenyan historians, stresses that Mau Mau was indeed a national movement.

The most controversial revision, and one which on the face of it has the least to do with history, concerns the attack on Dr Lynd's house in chapter 4. In the original version, this culminates not (only) in the brutal killing of her dog but in her rape by her houseboy, later revealed as Lieutenant K. This scene occupies a unique – though scarcely desirable – place in literature, as David Maughan Brown points out:

> To me, this scene suggests the ultimate extreme in attempts to provide 'both sides of the question'. It is worth emphasising again that this is the one account in all the fiction about 'Mau Mau' of the rape of a white woman by a freedom fighter, who is depicted in what is clearly intended to be a most distasteful light, and this is, ironically, because Ngugi is the most 'serious' of the writers.[45]

Removing the rape and Koinandu's obscene boasting which precedes it is perhaps no more than a straightforward attempt to make Koinandu (and hence Mau Mau) look better; it could also be due to Ngugi's later realisation of the limitations of a problematic ideal of 'balance' when writing about this type of subject.

There is an interesting parallel with the fact that, contemporaneously and equally egregiously, the English novelist Paul Scott was writing about the rape of a white woman by Indians in the context of anti-colonial struggles in *The Jewel in the Crown*. Again, the paradox is that it is Scott, the most pro-Indian of metropolitan novelists, who offers the only representation of such a rape. In both instances, there is the suggestion of a desire to utilise the concept of 'colonialism-as-rape'. In *A Grain of Wheat* that is indicated by Koinandu's thoughts 'Doing what you did to us – to black people', as he rapes Dr Lynd. However, as Maughan Brown points out, Koinandu's thoughts and emotions undermine this political reading of the rape. We might also link this undermining to the tendency in the novel, examined in more detail later, to explain and exonerate political actions via personal emotions, and to prioritise the latter over the former.

There is, however, a way in which rewriting the rape scene does have historical implications. Maughan Brown says 'the rape of Dr Lynd is simply the logical extreme in providing "the other point of view", where history becomes of no account.'[46] If balance for the sake of balance denies the real historical inequalities of power and violence, particularly here in the anti-colonial struggle, then giving up the balancing act is an important step towards the articulation of a more appropriate collective historical memory.

While in this kind of context Kenyatta's policy of burying the past, of 'forgive and (above all) forget', might appear aberrant, a profound betrayal of the culture and needs of the people, there is nevertheless a sense in which he could be seen to be following a powerful logic of modernity. According to one of the early analysts of the nation-state and national identity, Ernest Renan: 'Forgetting, and I would even go so far as to say historical error, is a crucial factor in the creation of a nation, which is why progress in historical studies often constitutes a danger for [the principle of] nationality.'[47] In such a perspective,

Kenyatta, as Father of the Nation, is arguably doing no more than is required of anyone in his founding and unifying position, inaugurating national forgetfulness and historical error for the sake of the nation. It is a moot point, of course, how far Renan is simply describing the predominant practices of Western nation-states, rather than enunciating an ineluctable iron law of their formation – or indeed the formation of non-Western ones. Ngugi, certainly, on the basis of later writings such as 'In Moi's Kenya, History is Subversive' in *Moving the Centre*, would want rather more of the 'progress in historical studies' Renan mentions, even at the (hypothetical) cost of creating a dangerous situation for the maintenance of national identity.

The problems of the depoliticising and dehistoricising role of the nationalist leader in the post-colonial context are perceptively analysed by Fanon:

> The leader, seen objectively, brings the people to a halt and persists in either expelling them from history or preventing them from taking root in it. During the struggle for liberation the leader awakened the people and promised them a forward march, heroic and unmitigated. Today, he uses every means to put them to sleep ...[48]

While Renan's analysis may have more of the feel of – or pretensions to being – a trans-historical law, Fanon's is very much based on a determinate set of historical events which should be learned from and not repeated in the process of building the post-colonial nation.

Ngugi's microcosm of the 'imagined community' of the nation is the more knowable one of the village of Thabai. In order to create a stronger feeling of closeness to that community, towards the end of the novel and particularly in the final section when the moment of Kenyan independence has arrived, he takes the unusual step of switching into a narrative voice in the first person plural:

> Somewhere a woman suggested we go and sing to Mugo, the hermit, at his hut ... For more than an hour, Mugo's hut was taken prisoner. His name was on everybody's lips.

> We wove new legends around his name and imagined
> deeds. We hoped that Mugo would come out and join us,
> but he did not open the door to our knocks. (204)

Although many readers have found this an effective device in
creating a sense of inclusiveness and shared identity, it does not
always please critics: the 'lack of narrative distance' which this
use of 'we' indicates for Nnolim in the article quoted earlier
represents, 'an artistic flaw that flies in the face of T. S. Eliot's
dictum that "the more perfect the artist, the more completely
separate in him will be the man who suffers and the mind which
creates".'[49] There is also the irony that while the positioning of
the narrative voice creates a stronger sense of the inclusive
community, the events of the narrative reveal a community
which could be regarded as even more fragmented than those in
the preceding novels (though a more optimistic reading would
see it as a community subject to divisive and destructive
pressures which it is in the process of overcoming).

The complex process of overcoming division and rebuilding
the community is embodied in the highly symbolic couple of
Gikonyo and Mumbi. They inevitably evoke the mythic primal
couple of Gikuyu and Mumbi, and what happens to them is
unavoidably linked to the narrative of the nation. Despite this
mythically and socially symbolic role, they are not reduced to
cyphers; rather, they function somewhat in the manner of
George Lukacs's famous theory of 'typical' characters in historical
fiction, where the particular stands in for the general. In order to
achieve proper realism (and nothing less will do for Lukacs)
'typical' characters in literature are required to be simultaneously fully developed and individualised, and able to represent
some larger collective entity – a class, or the nation. Gikonyo
and Mumbi carry their burden of representation, but they are
also very much themselves – indeed, the latter is so true of
Mumbi that it is tempting to see her as anything but a 'typical'
Gikuyu woman, as her power and pivotal role in the novel go
against received ideas (Western ones at least) of the behaviour of
African women. The painful reconstituting of the couple, and
the positive nature of Gikonyo's final version of the stool he will

carve as a belated wedding present for Mumbi, owe much to her strength, perseverance and courage. Her independent-minded behaviour – leaving Gikonyo because of his treatment of her and her baby – means that the reconstituted relationship will be more honest, while Gikonyo's decision to change the female figure in his carving to a pregnant one shows greater hope for the future than much of the narrative would give grounds for, not least as regards the national political dimension, where high level African corruption is already in operation.

While critics such as Nnolim may rail against Ngugi's 'forest of characters' and regard this as an unquestionable art-istic failing, there are grounds for seeing it as quite the opposite.[50] In *The Dialogic Imagination*, Bakhtin says that 'the novel must be a microcosm of heteroglossia'.[51] In other words, it must reproduce the diversity of languages and discourses which constitute the everyday reality of society. Also in Bakhtin's terms it should be very much a question of embodying this diversity of languages and speaking functions in characters. In such a perspective, Ngugi with his 'forest of characters' is trying hard to represent not only something of the diversity within the (national) community, but also the way in which the political struggle is instantiated in different discourses. At the level of the community, the range is from the almost speechless Mugo, via someone like Gikonyo for whom actions speak louder than words, to, at the opposite extreme, the endless, pointless, boast-ful chatter of Githua. It also encompasses the calm voice of traditional wisdom in Wambui and Warui, as well as the inspired and inspirational rhetoric of Kihika. On the other side of the colonial divide, there is the language of failed liberalism, in its instinctive or emotional mode in Dr Lynd, and its more 'philosophical' patronising form in John Thompson – the failure in each case producing a different language of denigration of Africans. In addition, what happens to the characters in relation to language or speech is important. Mugo's silence is the mark of a combination of alienation and guilt, and it is significant that in the end he finds both a voice and a sense of moral respons-ibility. Also, the fact that Gikonyo is brought to the point where he will discuss the previously unmentionable subject of Mumbi's child, as well as their future, is an element in the partial air of optimism on which the novel closes, even though, as Mumbi says, 'things are not so easy. What has passed between us is too much to be passed over in a sentence' (247). However, she does go on to add, 'we need to talk, to open our hearts to one another, examine them, and then together plan the future we want' (247). This typifies Mumbi's linguistic role in the novel – emotionally and factually honest, prepared to talk and to listen to anyone, thoughtful and concerned for others in what she says – she stands very much at the centre both of the linguistic spectrum of the novel and its moral and ethical structure.

Uncertainties notwithstanding, the general implications of the points in the preceding paragraphs seem reasonably clear: the nation (the people) can be relied upon to work things out for themselves, even though the apparatus of the nation-state may already be taken over and largely contaminated by the neo-colonialist black bourgeoisie. Certainly, the future of the (national) community appears ambiguous, unsure: the final utterance of the communal narrative voice is to record 'a disturbing sense of an inevitable doom' (217), about what is to come in the independence celebrations; at the same time, however, the community as embodied in the ordinary people has begun to confront and to discuss a range of problems regarding betrayal, retribution and forgiveness – and what comes after. The importance and the potential of these uncertain conjunctures, and the relation to them of indigenous writers, is expressed by Fanon:

> It is not enough to try to get back to the people in that past out of which they have already emerged; rather, we must join them in that fluctuating movement which they are just giving a shape to ... Let there be no mistake about it; it is to this zone of occult instability where the people dwell that we must come ...[52]

The complex and urgent dynamic which Fanon indicates, consisting of the people, their past, their present political choices, the setting in motion of their yet-to-be-established future, and the role of the writer in all this, is something which occupies Ngugi in the decade before the appearance of his next novel *Petals of Blood*.

The struggle betrayed

Petals of Blood

NGUGI'S fourth novel *Petals of Blood* continues and amplifies the sort of formal and ideological changes begun in *A Grain of Wheat*, and in so doing intensifies the divisions in the critical reception of his work.[1] It is the most demanding of his novels and the most politically outspoken to date, and attracted adverse criticism on the grounds of not being artistically successful (however that might be measured) or for 'dragging politics into art'. The fact that the latter point has been refuted again and again over the years (not least by the simple fact that no art, however much it might want to, can escape involvement in the political) still seems to constitute no obstacle to critics who happily incarnate the philosopher George Santayana's dictum 'those who cannot remember the past are condemned to repeat it.'[2] Once again (and unsurprisingly) questions of historical memory, the past and its (potential) problematic repetition are taken up by the novel. *Petals of Blood*'s treatment of history and the politics of historiography has made the latter the subject of bitter disagreement between Ngugi and a number of historians (Kenyan and Western) as we shall see later. The use of the past in the novel is certainly far more extensive than in earlier novels – given that almost the entire story is told in flashback – while questions relating to the past: how we understand it, the narratives we create of it, and the actions we base on it, form the central concerns of the book.

Itself an instance of cultural change, *Petals of Blood* is also a novel about cultural, political and personal change. It tells the story of the originally isolated rural community of Ilmorog, and of four individuals who come to it from outside: Munira the new schoolteacher; Abdulla the former Mau Mau fighter, disabled in the war and now a shopkeeper; Karega, the displaced social idealist, later political activist; and Wanja, former barmaid and prostitute, and victim of sexual exploitation. All of them have unresolved problems from the past which they are attempting to come to terms with or from which they are in flight. Their presence changes the community – eventually in profound ways – and they themselves are changed in the process, though not always for the better. Narrated in flashback from the standpoint of the 1970s, it is both the reconstruction of events leading up to a multiple murder and an overview of the last decade and more of Kenyan history, and brings Ngugi's ongoing narrative of Kenya up to the present. On the one hand, the book aligns itself with the popular genre of the detective novel in its guise of providing the solution to the murder mystery which opens the story; on the other, its epic dimensions and complex use of the past seem to place it more firmly in the camp of 'high' literature than Ngugi's other novels, and this encapsulates something of the internal division/complexity/artistic failing of the book (depending on one's point of view).

Something of that division could also be seen in the novel's combining of realist and symbolic elements. The style of the narrative is broadly realist, but the central quartet of characters, for instance, have definite emblematic significance, signalled, among other things, by their names: Karega (rebel) or Munira (stump). The latter not only indicates Munira's passivity, it also has significant historical implications – during the Mau Mau period, 'stump' was slang for informer or betrayer. The symbolism of naming extends to the other characters as well, such as the predatory Chui (leopard) or Nderi (vulture).

More substantially, the 'petals of blood' of the title constitute the centre of a symbolic chain which mirrors the transformations the narrative traces: from the bean flower found in the field in the 'innocent' early days and described by one of Munira's pupils as having petals of blood; to the *theng'eta* flower whose misuse and commodification both symbolically epitomises and is practically central to the growing invasion by capitalism; to Munira's arson attack on Wanja's brothel, 'the tongues of fire from the four corners forming petals of blood' (333), which marks, if not the end of an era, at least a significant moment with transformative potential; to Karega's final vision of the reign of the bloodthirsty monsters which must be swept away to create the opportunity for the flowering of full human existence. In turn, these form links in other chains: for example, Munira's arson attack is also the climax of a series of fires of greater or lesser severity connected with Wanja; and at the same time it is the repetition of his adolescent attempt to exorcise the guilt, frustration and shame experienced in relation to sex through a 'purificatory' act of arson (which just happens to be directed at the woman involved). In addition, at an early stage, the 'flower with petals of blood' becomes a sign of the dangers of involvement, of 'getting drawn in', for Munira. 'Involvement' is a deeply ambivalent process for him throughout the novel – he does everything he can to escape it, yet is unable to stop desiring it – and the final fiery flowering marks both the extent to which he has become involved and his inability to cope with that involvement.

Structurally, the novel is more complex than its pre-decessors. Divided into four (multiply subdivided) sections, it has two broad time frames – the narrative present of the ten days or so from the arrests to the solution of the crime, and the remembered past from Munira's arrival in Ilmorog twelve years previously – but is not contained by them. Moving backwards in time, there is colonial, pre-colonial and mythic history; moving forwards, there are events up to a month after the murders. Similarly, the narrative is broadly divided between the omniscient narrator and Munira's recollections, but is made more complex by characters telling their own stories and by the occasional appearance of a communal narrative voice, as in *A Grain of Wheat*.

The novel's complexity also exists at the level of connections. We have just seen something of that in relation to the ramifications of the 'petals of blood'; it continues at the level of the connectedness of the characters. Part of the fundamental impetus for the narrative is establishing connections, in terms of the police's efforts to assemble evidence and solve the crime. More important than the connections made by the police are those which the characters discover link them to one another in unexpected ways. For example, Munira learns that Karega had been in love with his sister Mukami, whose suicide Munira has never fully recovered from, and his jealousy leads to his fatal dismissal of Karega from his teaching post. It also transpires that Kimeria, one of the most ruthless capitalist exploiters in New Ilmorog and one of those who dies in Wanja's brothel, was the man who seduced Wanja as a child, and betrayed Karega's brother Nding'uri (the dearly loved Mau Mau comrade of Abdulla) to the British. These (and the examples could be multiplied) might seem like an excess of coincidence, but Ngugi is arguably making an important ideological statement – and one which critics generally prefer to ignore – concerning human inter-relatedness. Despite the fact that the central characters come to Ilmorog as apparently isolated individuals, and despite the fact that some, especially Munira, try to stay that way, profound and irrevocable connections exist. This image of connectedness is extended in Karega's final vision: despite social alienation, particularly as the result of capitalism, solidarity is not only possible but already exists, and truly human relations are there to be fought for and constructed.

As in the earlier novels, the focus of the narrative is the rural community confronting a particularly intense problem. Here, however, the problem has shifted from the forms or activities of colonialist domination – invasive or controlling – to one of colonialism's principal legacies in the shape of capitalist modernity: urbanisation; industrialisation; commodification of goods, processes and people; exploitation; class formation; the relentless pursuit of profit; rural depopulation and immiseration. The village and the city, Ilmorog and Nairobi, are originally presented as located in almost different worlds: geographically (the journey from Ilmorog to the city is virtually unimaginable for the ordinary people); historically (they instantiate different historical periods, especially in the narrative of 'development'); culturally (urban modernity involves profound changes in ways of living which include the threat – or fact – of cultural alienation); and ethically (many of the attitudes which allow or accompany the growth of capitalist modernity are at best foreign or incomprehensible, and at worst utterly repugnant, to ordinary Kenyans). To the extent that *Petals of Blood* narrates a collective tragedy, it is embodied in the ability of the city in all its ramifications to encroach upon and finally swallow the traditional and the rural.

This is not, however, a novel which is to be understood merely as an example of that opposition beloved of literary critics – 'tradition versus modernity'; nor is it the simple story of the loss of a rural paradise. Even before the narrative begins, Ilmorog has declined from what it once was (though the description of its past does tend towards an elevated or epic tone):

> Ilmorog, the scene of the unfolding of this drama, had not always been a small cluster of mud huts lived in only by old men and women and children, with occasional visits from wandering herdsmen. It had had its days of glory: thriving villages with a huge population of sturdy peasants who tamed nature's forests and, breaking the soil between their fingers, had brought forth every type of crop to nourish the sons and daughters of men. (120)

The irruption of modernity into Ilmorog is perceived archaically as the narrative gradually shifts in Chapter 2 from third person omniscient to the community voice, the collective 'we' encountered in *A Grain of Wheat*: 'But all that was twelve years after Godfrey Munira, a thin dust-cloud trailing behind him, first rode a metal horse through Ilmorog …' (5). This perspective is echoed later in the chapter: 'But it was the pressure lamp that later in the evening really captured our hearts and imaginations. Ilmorog star, we called it, and those who had travelled to beyond the boundary said it was very much like the town stars in Ruwa-ini, or the city stars that hang from dry trees' (31).

The existence of such perceptions in the 1960s shows, among other things, that the neo-colonial state is in no hurry to extend the trappings of modernity to all its citizens, and indeed the ignoring and undervaluing of rural areas by the state is one of the contributory factors in the famine which devastates Ilmorog. However, it is as a result of the drought and famine, and the epic journey of the Ilmorog villagers to Nairobi to ask for help from their MP, that modernity begins to reach Ilmorog – but for the wrong reasons. The corrupt MP Nderi wa Riera institutes the development of Ilmorog as a way of thwarting what he misinterprets as attempts to undermine his position. The process as it unfolds looks like a re-colonisation of the area: 'An administrative office for a government chief and a police post were the first things to be set up in the area. Next had come the church built by an Alliance of Missions as part of their missionary evangelical thrust into heathenish interiors' (195). Just as in colonialism proper, people lose their land – possibly with a slightly greater veneer of legitimacy than under colonial-ism, possibly not – and along with it their livelihood, though a few, repeating the pattern of past generations, manage to survive and, like Jacobo in *Weep Not, Child*, even become small-scale employers of people from their own community. Interest in Ilmorog is also fuelled by *theng'eta*, the potent ritual drink made for the village festival by Nyakinyua, subsequently sold on a small scale by Wanja and Abdulla, and later turned into a debased, mass-produced substance, manufactured in an industrial complex employing hundreds and sold to an international market. Although for a critic like Stuart Crehan this kind of account is simply sentimentalising and melodramatic, it is in fact a good illustration of the Marxist argument about the way in which capitalism turns use value (*theng'eta* made with care by people for their own use in important community ceremonies) into exchange value (*theng'eta* commercially produced simply as a commodity to be sold for the greatest possible profit).[3]

The physical transformation of Ilmorog is epitomised by

the Trans-Africa Highway, which not only divides the community in two, but is also not what the latter requires – as even Munira realises, smaller local roads would have been far more relevant to people's needs – and worst of all, it actually weakens the position of the region, the country, even the continent: 'And so, abstracted from vision of oneness, of a collective struggle of the African peoples, the road brought only the unity of the earth's surface: every corner of the continent was now within easy reach of international capitalist robbery and exploitation' (262) – as if international capitalism were needed, when the home-grown variety manages to exploit its people with such ruthlessness. The division of Ilmorog also replicates the profound class divisions which capitalism constructs, and for the first time in Ngugi's novels, we see the creation of the urban proletariat so important in Marxist analyses. It is the existence – and organisation – of the proletariat which provides the note of hope on which the novel ends. In response to the social fragmentation and expropriation which progress brings to Ilmorog, Wanja turns to organised prostitution, Abdulla turns to drink, and Munira turns to fundamentalist Christianity. For his part, Karega turns to militant trades union activism, becoming Secretary General of the Brewery Workers' Union, and it is partly as a result of his initiative that the workers of Ilmorog discover for the first time the power of their unity, with which to oppose the power of the bosses, and behind them the power of the neo-colonialist ruling class. While critics such as Crehan have attacked what they see as a view that only significant individuals or leaders can stir the masses and bring about political advances, it is notable that at the end of the novel the workers of Ilmorog are organising and taking decisions precisely without their imprisoned 'leader'. It is also significant that unlike Waiyaki, Njoroge or other characters in the earlier novels, Karega has no dreams of individual prominence – his hopes are all for collective emancipation, collectively realised.

The theme of betrayal which we have examined in earlier novels here reaches its most extreme and generalised form so far. The post-colonial bourgeoisie which constitutes the new ruling class in both economic and political terms is responsible for the wholesale betrayal of the hopes of the newly independent nation, the practical possibilities which independence offered, and the ideals of the national liberation struggle. The group which controls the 'development' of Ilmorog – three of whom are murdered in Wanja's brothel – is a cross-section of the compromised institutions of the new state: parliament (Nderi wa Riera), education (Chui the headmaster and Mzigo the administrator), the church (Rev. Jerrod Brown), and business (Kimeria). Some like Kimeria have very dark pasts (we mentioned his betrayal of Karega's brother and debauching of Wanja); others, like Chui, have turned their backs on more positive pasts; all are currently involved in the active exploitation of their fellow countrymen. In Nderi's case, this includes activities which are illegal as well as exploitative (smuggling precious stones, animal skins, and young women destined for foreign brothels) – a fact which the policeman in charge of the murder investigation realises, but, despite his belief in the need for a morally pure capitalism, declines to intervene in. In Kenyan terms, these men have not 'earned' their prominent positions through their efforts in the past – particularly when it is contrasted with what has been earned (but flagrantly withheld) namely the rewards for the sacrifices undertaken in the Mau Mau movement. Abdulla, who has lost a leg in the struggle, epitomises the attitude of the fighters:

> For weeks and months I kept on singing the song ['Kenya is a black man's country'] in anticipation / I waited for land reforms and redistribution / I waited for a job / I waited for a statue to Kimathi as a memorial to the fallen / I waited. (254)

The denial and dispossession of those who fought for freedom by those who did not will become one of Ngugi's enduring themes, as well as one of his principal accusations against the governments of post-colonial Kenya.

The denial and dispossession are based, among other things, on a rewriting of history, and in addition to their exploitative activities, Kimeria and his kind are involved in the production of a perverted picture of the past which both flatters and exonerates them all. Kimeria 'explains' to Karega:

> We used to have our little differences. He [Nderi] was what you might call a, eh, a freedom fighter, that is, he was a member of the party and was taken to detention. And I was, well, shall we say we didn't see eye to eye? Now we are friends. Why? Because we all realise that whether we were on that side of the fence or this side of the fence, or merely sitting astride the fence, we were all fighting for the same ends. Not so? We were all freedom fighters. (153)

The fact that this argument follows Kenyatta's official post-independence pronouncements on national reconciliation hardly makes it any the less repugnant. For Fanon, and perhaps even more so for Ngugi, the new black ruling class is unproductive, essentially parasitic, dependent upon foreign input. This is emphasised for instance in the growing involvement with tourism (Nderi has as colleague/accomplice in this field, the German who had tried to rape Wanja some years previously). The relationship is described by Karega as national prostitution, and is one which Ngugi has condemned on a number of occasions.

The fact that two of the most prominent betrayers of the people are also highly placed in the world of education is an index of the extent to which the latter has become a deeply problematic institution in the post-colonial world. *Petals of Blood* follows *The River Between* in having a teacher as a central character, but Munira is the opposite of Waiyaki's teacher-as-leader model: unable to act or decide, a permanent outsider, a mere observer of events, not even a participant. His approach to education also lacks any of the positive qualities of Waiyaki's, consisting as it does of the perpetuating of attitudes which served colonialism well, and now do the same for the neo-colonialist system. As he says to Karega: 'I say let's teach them facts, facts and not propaganda about blackness, African peoples, all that, because that is politics, and they know the tribe they belong to. That's a fact – not propaganda' (246). This view, apparently relevant to African needs and based on experience, is simply the recycling of what he has remembered from an English inspector's pamphlet and is shown by Karega to be wholly inadequate:

> Now let's look at this propaganda which is Not Facts. The oppression of black people is a fact. The scattering of Africans into the four corners of the earth is a fact ... That our people resisted European intrusion is a fact ... Our children must look at the things that deformed us yesterday, that are deforming us today. (246–7)

The realisation that there might be a continuity, even a complicity, between the deforming forces of yesterday and those of today is, however, one which few characters in the novel achieve.

The extent of the neo-colonial alienation of education is most forcefully embodied in Chui: intelligent, cultured, stylish and a leader of pupil resistance at the elite school of Siriana, he returns after independence to instigate a regime which is more oppressive than that operated by the British. That he does so in the face of student demands for autonomy and Africanisation which mirror those made on behalf of the nation reveals the power of neo-colonial co-optation. Despite this, educational success has not entirely lost its prestige in the novel: it is a matter of some importance that, having eventually gained access to education, Joseph does well, though there is an irony that his success occurs in the context of Siriana. One difference is that he, unlike Munira or Karega, has become politically aware – beyond the politics of the institution – while still at school. Against this it is important to set Karega's realisation, 'he had already started to doubt the value of formal education as a tool of people's total liberation' (252) (and not before time, one might think) which leads to a more fulfilling process of self-education. The simultaneous recognition of the severe limitations of institutionalised education under neo-colonialism, and the crucial importance of education in its broadest sense – socially relevant, politically liberating – is one which Karega shares with his author. The scope for relevant education to act as a source of empowerment for an individual, a community or a class is outlined in the collection *Barrel of a Pen*, written some years after *Petals of Blood*. Here, the desired end product accurately reflects what Karega becomes: 'The aim is to produce a producer, a thinker and a fighter all integrated in the same individual.'[4]

Karega's self-education is begun hopefully, but somewhat blindly: 'Karega did not know what it was that he really wanted to get, but he vaguely hoped for a vision of the future rooted in a critical awareness of the past. So he first tried the history books' (198). Attempting to find out about, to understand, or to come to terms with the past is a shared project for the novel as a whole (e.g., generically and structurally in terms of the invest-igation into the murders), as well as for its characters, who discover things about their own past, or other people's, their family's, or their country's. The past – in different ways – is a problem for all of the central characters, as it has increasingly become for the post-colonial nation. This is particularly true for Munira, and so it is appropriate that at the start of the novel we find him thinking, 'Lord, deliver us from our past' (7). Shortly after this, he explains his presence in Ilmorog in terms of atonement for the past: 'Some of us who had a schooling ... we tended to leave the struggle for Uhuru to the ordinary people. We stood outside ... the song, should I say. But now, with Independence, we have a chance to pay back ...' (10). Whether in fact such principled redemption of the past is Munira's aim is questionable, but his choice of the independence struggle as the symbol of the problematic past is important for the novel in general.

History and historiography constitute a particularly valorised way of understanding the past, so it is logical that Karega should begin his studies there. It is also a particularly sensitive area in post-colonial Kenya, and one in which Ngugi has intervened on a number of occasions. Karega realises the shortcomings of historians – not least those Africans who refuse either to discuss the real implications of colonialism and imperialism or to represent African history other than in those terms of primitiveness and aimlessness long favoured in the West. Wanja's comment to Karega: 'Sometimes there is no greatness in the past. Sometimes one would like to hide the past even from oneself' (128), is first and foremost a reference to her own unsatisfactory life, but it is also unmistakably the product of dominant representations of the African past which undermine belief in one's culture.

On one level, Karega's disillusionment with African historians could appear to be simply a narrative device, providing a stage in his progress to 'truer' forms of knowledge and, above all, the eventual blending of theory and practice in revolutionary activism. It also involves a changed view of the past and how to use it, an acknowledgement of the insufficiency of merely recognising the existence of the former greatness Wanja longed for. The terms of Karega's conversion might have come straight from the pages of *The Wretched of the Earth*:

> Even in himself he could not recognise the dreamer who once could talk endlessly about Africa's past glories, Africa's great feudal cultures, as if it was enough to have this knowledge to cure one day's pang of hunger, to quench an hour's thirst or clothe a naked child. (301)

On a rather different level, this, apparently no more than an academic disagreement over historical detail, is the sign both of an individual struggle by Ngugi, and a more general one by intellectuals in post-colonial Kenya, in what the German critic Walter Benjamin might have called 'a fight for the oppressed past'. Historians such as J. M. Kariuki and Maina wa Kinyatti, and writers like Ngugi himself, have opposed the deeply negative versions of the African past, and closer to home, have resisted both the rewriting of the history of Mau Mau and the astonishing efforts by the government to eradicate it from the life of the nation and from popular memory by banning commemorative events and suppressing books about the period.[5] Among the aspects of Mau Mau which Ngugi stresses is its national character. On the one hand this is in opposition to standard British colonial explanations of the war as simply the expression of frustrated Gikuyu tribalism and the result of their inability to adapt to modernity. On another level, it reflects both Ngugi's long-term opposition to the extreme divisiveness of the discourse of tribalism in Kenya, and to the effects of excessive ethnic chauvinism, as well as his concern at the manipulation of these negative forces by the Moi regime. Also, claims for the national character of Mau Mau allow Ngugi to align Kenyan resistance to the British firmly with other, indisputably national, liberation struggles of the kind theorised by Cabral, Fanon and others.

The attempt to create and exploit ethnic chauvinism is represented in the novel by Nderi wa Riera's KCO (Kikuyu Central Organisation). While the psychology of the circumstances of its inception – a sudden inspirational decision to set it up to forestall movements against him in the Ilmorog district – might appear unlikely, the coercive way in which it operates has clear parallels with the post-independence use of KANU by Kenyatta to make money and enforce loyalty to his rule.

Although Ngugi's interpretation of Mau Mau is officially rejected in Kenya for obvious reasons, it also fails to find favour with some Western historians, even those who would be broadly sympathetic to his aims. In *Unhappy Valley*, their lengthy analysis of colonial Kenya, Berman and Lonsdale, who claim left-wing affiliation, accuse Ngugi and others classed as 'radicals' of being cavalier with historical facts:

> Ideal heroism has been most determinedly demanded of the evidence by those who have least studied it, who can indeed sneer at those who bury Mau Mau 'in a heap of footnotes'. Kenyan liberals have protested against this contempt for authorised professional standards, calling it 'intellectual terrorism'.[6]

The choice of 'terrorism' here is interesting, given that the actual terrorism has been state-sponsored: the assassination of J. M. Kariuki, the imprisonment of Maina wa Kinyatti, and the imprisonment and exile of Ngugi indicate the high price of (historically informed) dissent and resistance in post-colonial Kenya, and that arguments over the past can be literally deadly.

The development of resistance in the novel is another of the areas where coming to terms with the past is important. The growing awareness that earlier generations had fought for their freedom from a variety of oppressors makes similar behaviour more imaginable for those suffering oppression in the present. If that is true of the distant past, it is even more true of the recent past through which people have lived, and which still impinges on their lives. For instance, stories of the Mau Mau, of Dedan Kimathi, and significantly, of the part played by ordinary people like Abdulla, help to give the deputation from Ilmorog the resolve to undertake their mission to the city.

A different kind of lived relation to the past is embodied in Nyakinyua, the most extensively represented of the original inhabitants of Ilmorog, and the most representative of positive aspects of older forms of Kenyan culture. She carries a range of cultural and historical knowledge, and is able, for example, to pass on the secrets of the method of making *theng'eta* (with its unforeseen consequences for the community), or to tell stories about the mythic and historical past of Ilmorog to hearten the villagers on their trek to the city, or to outsmart Njuguna in the erotic antiphonal singing games of the circumcision ceremony, or to sing movingly of struggle and resistance not only as the recollection of past events, but also as a continuing responsibility for the youth of the community. It is her explanation of her husband's experiences and death under colonialism which helps Wanja to come to terms with her family's past, and Wanja subsequently sacrifices almost everything in order to buy Nyakinyua's hut after the old woman's death. (Critical opinion, it has to be said, divides over whether this is a positive characterisation recuperating important traditional social roles, or whether it is over-idealised and sentimentalised.)

Nyakinyua and her stories instantiate an older generation's ways of resisting. New times call forth new forms and strategies. In particular, the alliance of so-called former opponents outlined by Kimeria which now constitutes the ruling elite in Kenya is confronted by the emergent post-colonial alliance of peasants and the new urban proletariat. The latter, awakening to the sense of the power contained in their unity and organisation, inaugurate a new era and provide the basis for Karega's final apocalyptic/utopian vision:

> Tomorrow it would be the workers and the peasants leading the struggle and seizing power to overturn the system of all the preying bloodthirsty gods and gnomic angels, bringing to an end the reign of the few over the many and the era of drinking blood and feasting on human flesh. Then, only then, would the kingdom of man and woman really begin, they joying and loving in creative labour ... (344)

The indefinite postponement of the joyous loving kingdom of man and woman is no doubt one reason for the unsatisfactory nature of male–female relations in the novel. Munira, for example, finds satisfaction neither with his wife, nor Lillian, nor Wanja; Karega similarly fails with Munira's sister and with Wanja; Abdulla seems never to have had a lasting relationship, while Wanja herself is the epitome of a restless search for love, emotional stability and fulfilment. Prostitution, as a (growing, especially urban) social practice and a (symbolic) national condition, similarly hardly constitutes grounds for happy and fulfilling relations. At the sexual/emotional centre of the novel is Wanja, the reluctant but hugely successful prostitute, who, if she lacks something of the uncompromised goodness of Mumbi in *A Grain of Wheat*, nevertheless occupies an even more pivotal role in the narrative. By the latter stages she stands literally and symbolically between two opposed groups of men, Kimeria, Chui and Mzigo, and Karega, Munira and Abdulla, in some ways keeping them apart (trying, for instance, to warn Karega or protect him from the violent intentions of the opposing triumvirate), but also uniting them, not least in the fact that she has slept with them all. Wanja also introduces the theme of sexual exploitation and revenge which is important for Ngugi – and not just for Ngugi: it is powerfully reworked, for example,

in Djibril Diop Mambety's recent film *Hyenes*, where the sentiments expressed by the central character Ramatou: 'Society
made me a whore; now I'm going to make the whole world a
brothel', would find an echo in Wanja. The fact that Wanja is
able to achieve spectacular revenge on the exploiters at an
individual level also prefigures the revolutionary possibility for
the exploited nation to bring about the kind of changes envi-
sioned by Karega.

Wanja's revenge represents something of a belated transformation, or recognition of the truth of things on her part.
Prior to that, her earlier efforts to escape from prostitution and
make an 'honest' living via the bar and restaurant having failed,
she has seemingly been increasingly drawn into a sexualised
version of the dominant ethos of the post-colonial state: 'This
world ... this Kenya ... this Africa knows only one law. You eat
somebody or you are eaten. You sit on somebody or somebody
sits on you' (291). Turning the conditions of her original oppression (being a woman and therefore sexually vulnerable, if not
automatically 'available'), into the conditions of her material
success (becoming rich and influential in New Ilmorog thanks to
her flourishing brothel), represents a kind of victory for Wanja,
though she is, nevertheless, still operating within the conditions
laid down by a corrupt system. However, her greater victory
over her oppressors and the conditions of her oppression, and
one which signals a profound change of attitude on her part, is
achieved by the triple murder (even though that was not what
she had planned).

The gendering and sexualising (and allegorising) of questions
of national liberation is of course a contentious issue. Although
Ngugi's portrayal of women has been praised, including by
feminists, other critics have argued that it is still ideologically
bound up with patriarchy. In *Contemporary African Literature
and the Politics of Gender*, Florence Stratton suggests that

> In these texts [by Ngugi, Soyinka, Ousmane and many
> others] prostitution is not related to the female social
> condition in patriarchal societies. Rather it is a metaphor
> for men's degradation under some non-preferred socio-

political system – a metaphor which encodes women as agents of moral corruption, as sources of moral contamination in society.[7]

The use of women's sexual oppression merely as a more exciting image of men's social oppression is clearly unacceptable, but it is difficult to see that as in any way what Ngugi is doing here. As previously mentioned, Karega argues that the whole nation is prostituted, but this makes it a problem for everyone, not just men. Similarly, there are some examples in the novel which might seem to support the 'moral contamination' argument – a popular song which praises a woman but ends with the words 'but oh, darling / What poison you carry between your legs'; Kimeria telling Wanja that she bewitched him, when in fact he debauched her; Munira's growing and ultimately lethal obsession (born of sexual frustration and perverted Christianity) with Wanja as likely to ensnare and corrupt Karega – but these hardly carry much authority, and indeed, are more significant precisely as symptoms of the social conditions which so violently oppress women.

Stratton also suggests that, along with all the other male writers who use the 'Mother Africa' trope she is criticising, 'Ngugi [associates] Wanja with the heritage of African values – values that are timeless, impervious to history.'[8] Again, this is difficult to see in the novel, firstly because if there is a single repository of traditional African values, it is Wanja's grandmother Nyakinyua, rather than Wanja herself (since, even though it could perhaps be argued that sacrificing everything to save her grandmother's hut from the property developers constitutes a taking up of her traditional position, Wanja is far too representative of 'modern' womanhood); secondly, because in a novel so concerned with history and the question of social change, the notion of timeless values would be, at the very least, extremely paradoxical. Despite this, Stratton's critique alerts us to the presence of possible contradictions in the practice of writers even when they are apparently at their most aware or progressive.

Part of Stratton's argument is the entirely sensible proposition that even though writers like Ngugi and Ousmane are praised for their progressive politics, that does not prevent their novels from (unwittingly) purveying reactionary ideologies. This kind of actual or potential disjuncture recalls Bakhtin's distinction between progressive writers and progressive works. Bakhtin, for instance, regarded Tolstoy's novels as monologic – and hence not progressive – because of the degree of authorial control of character and discourse, whereas Dostoyevsky's more open, polyphonic novels he considered progressive. This was despite the political positions of the two men, Tolstoy holding by far the more radical beliefs. The same kind of Bakhtinian question can be asked in relation to *Petals of Blood*. If *A Grain of Wheat* represents something of a transition from the early dialogism of *The River Between*, *Petals of Blood* is a much more fully realised polyphonic novel, with a more open structure and above all a diversity of voices: omniscient narration, and inclusive 'we' narration; a range of characters telling their own stories. However, although as a polyphonic novel *Petals of Blood* would be progressive in Bakhtin's terms, according to Stratton it is not progressive because it reproduces patriarchal ideologies. Bakhtin saw the novel as endlessly questioning or relativising dominant ideologies and official discourses through its deployment of a range of other voices and discourses, and this, we could argue, is what *Petals of Blood* does with capitalism and neo-colonialism (and patriarchy): allowing their premises to be articulated, but exposing them to critique from the variety of differently-located voices and ideological positions represented by Abdulla, Karega, Wanja or Nyakinua – even though not all these voices tend in exactly the same direction. (It may of course be the case that readers feel that patriarchy remains more of a blind spot for Ngugi than the other more obviously 'political' targets of colonialism and imperialism.)

Even at his most individualistic (for instance in *The River Between* or *Weep Not, Child*) Ngugi never blames individuals for the problems of the community or nation in the way that Achebe tends to do. Nevertheless, *Petals of Blood* marks an interesting shift in terms of locating both responsibility and power. Although, as we have seen, the levers of power in Kenya are clearly held by the black neo-colonial elite, they are in effect no more than intermediaries: at best self-serving middlemen, at worst puppets whose strings are pulled by the immeasurably more powerful and faceless system of capitalism, operating in its global mode as imperialism. It is this greater awareness of the systemic nature of the problems facing Kenya which marks the shift in *Petals of Blood*. Even Wanja's father recognises

> The true secret of the white man's power: money. Money moves the world. Money is time. Money is beauty. Money is elegance. Money is power. Why, with money I can even buy the princess of England … With money I can buy freedom for all our people. (233)

Although his understanding is rudimentary and his faith in the possibility of purchasing freedom is wildly misplaced, he is nevertheless broadly correct. A less euphoric view, and another fundamental error, is voiced by the lawyer:

> We could have done anything, then, because our people were behind us. But we, the leaders, chose to flirt with the molten god, a blind, deaf monster who has plagued us for hundreds of years. We reasoned: what is wrong is the skin-colour of the people who ministered to this god: under our own care and tutelage we shall tame the monster and make it do our will. We forgot that it has always been deaf and blind to human woes. So we go on building the monster and it grows and waits for more, and now we are all slaves to it. (163)

If the earlier underestimation of capitalism was at fault, the lawyer's current analysis of it is correct: capitalism is indeed colour-blind; it could in theory be taken over and run by Africans for their benefit; it is also (monstrously) relentless in its demands. His semi-mythic tale does, however, echo more sober academic assessments: in *Historical Capitalism*, for example, theorist and historian Immanuel Wallerstein highlights both the profoundly illogical (and relentless) nature of capitalism, 'far from being a "natural" system, as some apologists have tried to argue, historical capitalism is a patently absurd one. One accumulates capital in order to accumulate more capital', as well as its lack of concern for the human cost involved: 'The overwhelming proportion of the world's work-forces who live in rural zones or move between them and urban slums, are worse off than their ancestors five hundred years ago.'[9]

Although the lawyer's imagistic presentation and Karega's final vision might diminish the seriousness of their economic and political assessments in the eyes of some readers, the former does at least speak to his largely rural audience in an idiom with which they would be familiar, and both of them echo classic Marxist formulations such as the following: 'Only then [after "a great social revolution"] will human progress cease to resemble that hideous pagan idol, who would not drink the nectar but from the skulls of the slain.'[10] While some critics regard Karega's final vision, or indeed the whole concluding section of the novel, as artistically flawed, from another perspective that may be an indication of their own shortcomings:

> But this is not to argue that narrative is merely 'illusory', any more than we should chide the working class movement for nurturing its mighty dreams of universal solidarity overcoming the evils of capitalism. Such motifs are the necessary inflections by which the theory of historical materialism 'lives itself out' in the practice of class struggle. And just as the individual subject is permitted to construct for itself a coherent biography, so a revolutionary or potentially revolutionary class creates, across the structurally discontinuous social formations identified by Marxism, that 'fiction' of a coherent, continuous struggle which is Benjamin's 'tradition'.[11]

This is an argument with important implications for the reading, and evaluation, of certain types of fiction. For some readers, the question would no doubt remain whether, even allowing for structural or political necessity, there are still grounds for aesthetic doubts about this or other aspects of the novel. There is also the question of whether, however much he might welcome this kind of theoretical support, Ngugi might still want to argue for the reality, rather than the fictionality, of the 'coherent, continuous struggle'.

A different perspective on what, for Ngugi, has been the high point of that struggle is provided by the play *The Trial of Dedan Kimathi*. Published the year before *Petals of Blood*, *The Trial of Dedan Kimathi* represents an intervention in that kind of historiography which, as we have seen, Karega and his author deplore, as well as in the enforced historical amnesia of contemporary Kenya. It is therefore not without significance that Ngugi and his co-author Micere Mugo offer a much longer than usual preface explaining the thinking behind the text, the kind of questions which prompted it – whether, for instance, the theme of Mau Mau was now exhausted, or whether, on the contrary, it had ever been adequately treated in Kenyan literature. Researching the play showed Ngugi and Micere Mugo not only how important the memory of Kimathi still was to the people of his area, but also that direct personal knowledge contradicted standard or official accounts of the man (for instance, that Kimathi had acquired military skill through having served with the British in World War 2, rather than, as now appeared to be the case, from his own abilities and the circumstances of the independence struggle against the British). The Kimathi play was envisaged as just the first in a series which would resurrect the history of Kenyan resistance to foreign invaders – again highlighting the importance of a sense of connection and continuity, with Mau Mau as only the latest example of Kenyans' refusal to accommodate themselves to foreign occupation (whatever certain Kenyan historians might be arguing) as well as part of a continent-wide, ultimately worldwide, movement of anti-colonial resistance. In a way which perhaps inevitably recalls Brecht's well-known statements on the subject, the authors abandon a literal approach to realism: 'The play is *not* a reproduction of the farcical "trial" at Nyeri', in order to achieve a better realism: 'So the challenge was to truly depict the masses (symbolised by Kimathi) in the only historically correct perspective: positively, heroically and as the true makers of history.'[12]

Instead of the detail of the legalistic process, we see Kimathi undergoing four 'trials' or attempts to break his resolve, which are more reminiscent of the temptation of Christ. In the first of these, the symbolically multi-purpose British official Shaw Henderson, who acts as judge, prosecutor, etc. (and who bears the surname of the policeman who captured the real Kimathi) offers Kimathi his life in exchange for a confession which would bring the fighting to an end. In the second, members of the African and Asian middle class tempt Kimathi with visions of material wealth. In the third, a politician, a priest, and a former 'radical' now a successful businessman, try to convince him that the people's demands have been met and that there is nothing left to fight for. The fourth and final trial is rather more unconvincing as Henderson tries to torture Kimathi into signing a letter telling the remaining Mau Mau fighters to surrender. Kimathi, however, overcomes the trials of doubts and weakness, reaffirms his refusal, is 'tried' and sentenced to death. Despite that, the play ends on a particular note of defiance and hope which is the trademark of the later Ngugi: his faith in the continuing resistance of Kenyan people restored, Kimathi is led off to his death, but his example lives on, with the boy and the girl proclaiming him 'not dead' in the manner of the best mythological and folk heroes. The play humanises Kimathi in opposition to received versions of him as a ruthlessly efficient – or simply ruthless – Mau Mau leader (or, in his captor Ian Henderson's contemporary account, *The Hunt for Kimathi*, crazed, brutal, bloodthirsty and irrational). Here it is his generosity of spirit in pardoning the traitors, who include his brother, which is central to his downfall, and which – sparing him too much of the superhuman – could be seen as a very basic error on his part. Once again, we enter the space of revisionist historiography as political struggle: for Ngugi, as we have already seen, the official trial was a farce, while the impromptu trial of the Mau Mau traitors is characterised by democratic debate among the guerrillas and leniency on Kimathi's part. For Henderson, unsurprisingly, it was the opposite: 'It [Kimathi's official trial] had been a fair and thorough trial by any standard. It was quite a contrast with his "trials" in the forest.'[13] 'Indeed,' Ngugi would no doubt reply.

Woven around all this is the story of 'the boy', 'the girl' and 'the woman', partly to provide an image of ordinary people's involvement in the struggle – acting as messengers, look-outs, couriers and even would-be rescuers (the motif of the gun hidden in the loaf of bread also appears in Ngugi's children's book *Njamba Nene's Pistol*) – and partly as a narrative of maturation and assumption of moral responsibility resulting from the involvement. Another aspect of the representation of a broader social sweep is the portrayal of tableau-style events from black people's history (slavery, the arrival of colonialism, colonial oppression), as well as, in much more detail, moments from the Mau Mau war involving Kimathi. Although some of these moments are enacted in a broadly realistic manner, the text is always likely to veer off – for example in the scene where the boy and the girl fight, but the boy is restrained by the disembodied voice of the woman reminding him of the process of understanding and responsibility he is engaged in.

The latter is typical of the importance of the woman in the play: as catalyst of the action (for example, in getting the boy to carry the gun), or as centre of moral authority (for example, in her stand on male-female relations, and on involvement in the struggle). Interestingly, she sees more clearly than Kimathi the need, in the context of the war, not to be hampered by questions of blood relationship in determining who one's real allies and enemies are. (Compare the British view in Henderson: 'Mau Mau had taught him, like all others who succumbed to its doctrine, to have no feelings for kith and kin.'[14]) It is not surprising that Kimathi declares: 'When this struggle is over / We shall erect at all the city corners / Monuments / To our women / Their courage and dedication / To our struggle.'[15]

The Trial of Dedan Kimathi is very much a transitional text: Ngugi's first collaborative project (jointly written, but with input from a number of others), it is his last play written in English and makes more extensive use of Gikuyu – from the opening and closing songs to the street vendors' cries, or the interrogation of suspects – though Ngugi was aware of the contradictions (as he later says in *Decolonising the Mind*) in representing people's speech in this artificially hybrid manner. In the meantime, people speak good English for good Gikuyu.

In terms of power relations, the play offers a straightforward opposition between indigenous insurgency and the forces of British colonialism (military, judicial and 'loyal', i.e. African collaborationist) and though the latter 'win' because Kimathi is captured and killed, the evidence of popular resistance indicates that they will not always be victorious.

Devil on the Cross

One of the central themes of *Petals of Blood* is the complex relation of continuity and change; that could also be said to describe the relation between *Petals of Blood* and its successor *Devil on the Cross*. However, even coming from a writer whose approach to his craft has always involved change and adaptation, *Devil on the Cross* appeared to a number of readers to involve disorienting shifts. Some of these – the form of the narrative; the language in which it is written – involved conscious decisions on Ngugi's part; others – most notoriously, the practical circumstances of its writing – involved factors over which he had no control. *Devil on the Cross* is famous for having been written in secret on toilet paper during Ngugi's year of imprisonment without trial (often in solitary confinement) in Kamiti Maximum Security Prison during the (literally) dying months of the Kenyatta regime.

For Ngugi's novel-reading public, *Devil on the Cross* could indeed look like a major change of direction: written in Gikuyu; framed as a ritualised performance of *gicaandi*; broadly, even obscenely, satirical in tone and content; drawing heavily on techniques of traditional orature, as well as indigenous forms of proverbs, fables and myth. Nevertheless, in many fundamental ways the novel is a continuation of a number of aspects of Ngugi's evolving literary practice. For example, although it is –

shockingly for some – written in Gikuyu (an issue to which we shall return later in the chapter) Ngugi had already co-authored and produced a play *Ngaahika Ndeenda* (*I Will Marry When I Want*) in Gikuyu for the Kamiriithu Community Theatre Group. In addition, its major themes can be found in other forms in the earlier novels. Even its striking departures from novelistic verisimilitude are foreshadowed in *Petals of Blood*. For instance, the way in which characters' names in the earlier novel function as allegorical labels indicating moral status: Cambridge Fraudsham, Sir Swallow Bloodall, or emblematic status: Karega (rebel), Wanja (stranger), is continued, and exaggerated, in *Devil on the Cross*, partly in line with the awfulness of the character: Mweri wa Mukiraai (self-promoter, son of he who silences people), Kihaahu wa Gatheeca (madman, son of glutton), or Gitutu wa Gataanguru (inhuman one, son of tapeworm). In keeping with the tone of *Devil on the Cross*, exaggeration becomes outrageous: Gitutu's baptismal name is Rottenborough Groundflesh Shitland Narrow Isthmus Joint Stock Brown – which, as he says, makes Europeans look at him strangely. There is continuity, too, in the (imaginary) geography of the novel. The story concerns a group of people who travel in a *matatu* taxi to Ilmorog – invented location of *Petals of Blood*, and paradigmatic community of post-colonial Kenya – and the disparate and sometimes painful reasons which bring them to Ilmorog (escaping, searching, going home) carry echoes of the central characters in *Petals of Blood*. At the same time, they are all variously drawn to the event which is the novel's satirical centrepiece, the feast and competition in international theft and robbery being organised in Ilmorog. Even more than the central quartet in *Petals of Blood*, the occupants of the *matatu* are a representative cross-section of modern Kenyan society – the driver, Robin Mwaura, self-seeking and materialistic; Wangari, a country woman who fought in the Mau Mau movement; the young intellectual Gatuiria who is in the process of discovering his cultural roots; the politicised worker Muturi; the educated businessman Mweri wa Mukiraai; Wariinga, a secretary and 'modern' young woman. Their life histories up to that point are representative fragments of the post-colonial nation-state, but their lives are profoundly altered by the events in and around the competition.

Another aspect of continuity and change in the novel is the way in which it offers something like a second chance, a set of circumstances repeated from the previous novel but with a different outcome. For instance, Wariinga, like Wanja, is seduced by an older man, has a baby and is abandoned; unlike Wanja, however, she neither kills her baby nor slides into a life of bar work and prostitution, though like Wanja she returns to Ilmorog (family, the country) when the pressures of urban life become intolerable. However, the fact that unlike Wanja she does not make herself sexually available (either habitually or professionally) means that she is subject to relentless male demands.

The representation of gender is one area where having a second chance does not necessarily mean getting it right – at least for Ngugi, and it remains one of the most contentious aspects of his novels. While Wariinga spectacularly 'gets it right' (far too much for some critics) in terms of the successful transformation of her life, in the eyes of some feminist critics her creator fails, at the ideological level at least, to equal that process of successful change. Although between *Petals of Blood* and *Devil on the Cross* Ngugi made a number of statements regarding the need for improvement in the position of women in society, and although as he explains in *Detained* his vision of Wariinga was both the impetus for the novel and one of the things which sustained him in prison, his treatment of her still seems to some to display patriarchal ideological affiliations. When the novel opens, Wariinga has just suffered a triple blow at the hands of men: sacked because she will not sleep with her boss; ditched by her boyfriend (on the grounds that she is sleeping with her boss) because she will no longer be able to support him financially; and thrown out of her room by her landlord when she refuses to pay the increased rent. Intending simply to return to Ilmorog to her family, she, along with the other passengers, attends the Devil's Feast, and as a result of events there, she, like Wanja at the end of *Petals of Blood*, questions where she stands in relation to social issues and injustice. In the following two years she is completely transformed as she sheds her former subservience to patriarchal concepts of female beauty and female capability, both intellectually and professionally. Newly confident and determined not to surrender, she triumphs over sexism in a variety of forms: studying engineering at the Polytechnic, she gets a job in a cooperatively run garage by demonstrating knowledge superior to that of one of the mechanics; studying karate at a martial arts club allows her to deal forcibly with a customer who fondles her while she works on his car. While many critics have seen the transformation of Wariinga as ideologically very positive (if not necessarily tremendously credible) others have, as mentioned, still found the representation of her objectionably patriarchal. Florence Stratton, for example, accuses Ngugi of masculinising Wariinga through her choice of profession, saying, 'in Ngugi's conception, secretaries are not "workers", a concept which he defines from an exclusively male perspective ...', even though that would appear to be directly contradicted by Ngugi's account of his time in Kamiti prison, where he and other inmates 'often discussed women of different careers, especially barmaids, secretaries and engineers'.[16] However odd the list, it would seem that secretaries and engineers hold equal status in Ngugi's scheme of things. Also, rather than simply masculinising her because masculine somehow equals better, the transformation of Wariinga arguably has more to do with affirming the notion that an individual could possess masculine and feminine qualities and do things associated with both, without thereby becoming 'unnatural'. Stratton also accuses Ngugi of purveying an unrealistic view of gender equality in peasant and working class society, when all he has done is to say that Wariinga wins the respect of her fellow workers through her ability – an individualised circumstance, not a generalised claim. There is also a sense in which an argument based on criteria of strict mimeticism is not the most relevant to a text whose stance on reality and novelistic realism is, as we shall see, less than straightforward.

Certainly, Wariinga's battle against sexual exploitation, especially as practised by older and more powerful men, is indicative of a social problem in Kenya. Ingrid Bjorkman reports a debate in the Kenyan parliament when a woman MP tried to introduce a bill to force men to contribute to the upkeep of their illegitimate children. Responses from male MPs included:

> If she gets pregnant, that is up to her, because she had weighed herself. Why should I accept responsibility for a child born out of wedlock?
>
> Before any woman agrees to sleep with a man, she should differentiate whether that is for a few minutes, one day, or for marriage. It is the woman who makes the decision. My work, as a man, is to plant the seed and quit.[17]

The irresponsible, predatory sexism of the ruling class could hardly have been better delineated by Ngugi himself. The shifting of all the blame on to the woman, the idea that men's work is limited to impregnating and disappearing, are particularly significant. Novels such as *Devil on the Cross* highlight the irrelevance of women deciding or hoping that it is 'for marriage', given the ability of men simply to 'quit'.

Elleke Boehmer, in what is perhaps the best short analysis of Ngugi's representation of women, is also critical of his treatment of gender issues, though her comments are often more to the point than Stratton's. However, even Boehmer arguably goes too far in her negative assessment: 'Ngugi's neglect of both the gendered and the structural nature of power, whether that power is held by national or by proletarian forces, ultimately works to inhibit his rousing call for a new dispensation in Kenya.'[18] From what we have seen so far in this study, understanding of the structural nature of power would in fact appear to be one of Ngugi's stronger points, while its gendered dimension clearly constitutes a growing awareness. 'Simply expressed, the problem would rather seem to be an identification of national freedom with male freedom and an inherited state structure. Thus a patriarchal order survives intact.'[19] Here again, although the former point highlights a blind spot of (male) nationalist and anti-colonial thought (and one of which the younger Ngugi is no doubt guilty) it is hard to see it as an unchanged component of his thought, in the light of both the type of representation of female characters in his later novels, and the specific articulation of calls for women's emancipation. The issue of the inherited state structure is similarly partially correct. Nationalist thought, as Fanon was well aware, had great difficulty rethinking, or thinking beyond the forms of the nation-state. The combination of overt Marxism (which *ought* not to leave the state structure intact) and Pan Africanism (which at least *claims* to move beyond national boundaries) in the later Ngugi again makes such a non-evolving approach unlikely.

Elleke Boehmer's comments return us to an examination of power in *Devil on the Cross*, and what we find is an intensification of the mass or class dimension, and paradoxically of the individual component. The hold of the black capitalist class in Kenya is stronger than before, but is even more visibly a derivative power, given or withheld by the international capitalists, and the arrogance of Kenyan capitalists towards their own people is matched only by their grovelling to their foreign masters (the Kenyan master of ceremonies at the Feast declaring that they are the willing slaves of the foreign capitalists). Their dreams are of an even greater exploitative use of their power (such as selling the very air to workers in their country and withholding it if the workers step out of line) and their gathering in Ilmorog is to boast of their ability to exploit in the hope of being given more power to do so. The apogee of their dystopian imaginings is to make literally true what is so far true only in a more metaphorical sense, and steal, and make profit from, the blood, sweat and strength of the workers, siphoning them off and selling them abroad. Despite their desire to be internationally respectable 'thieves and robbers', as Mweri wa Mukiraai points out, they have no power whatsoever beyond their national borders, even though they do possess enormous repressive as well as exploitative power within those borders.

Against them is ranged that power which is only just beginning to be aware of itself: the united resistance of all the groups exploited by the capitalist class. Wanja's world of 'eat or be eaten' in *Petals of Blood* is one which capitalists now want to portray as two separate ones, the eaters and the eaten, each of them 'natural' and inevitable, hiding the fact that – as Satan's voice tells Wariinga – there is a third possibility, a revolutionary world where the old order will be overturned, and it is this which 'the Holy Trinity of the worker, the peasant and the patriot' (230) aim to create.

The 'blatantness' of *Devil on the Cross*, its various excesses, and lack of concern for decorum and novelistic niceties, could be viewed as an intervention in a particular ruse of power. In 'Multiculturalism, or The Cultural Logic of Multinational Capitalism', Slavoj Zizek comments on the way in which self-censorship helps power to operate more efficiently.[20] Using Zizek's idea, we can see self-censorship at work both in the dominant group in society and in the dominated. At a certain level, we all know that capitalism exploits us all for all of our working lives, that manual workers are more exploited than most, that Third World peasants and workers are frequently exploited far beyond the bounds of human decency, yet we choose not to face this knowledge openly, or in a sustained manner, effectively censoring ourselves, thereby allowing the system to operate freely, and helping to create something akin to the 'friction-free capitalism' envisaged by Bill Gates of Microsoft. At the same time, the capitalist class censors itself by not articulating the (almost literally unspeakable) truth of capitalism, its methods and effects – the fact that, while the countries of the European Union will gain enormously from the effects of the latest round of GATT (General Agreement on Tariffs and Trade) decisions, and while other areas may be relatively little affected, Sub-Saharan Africa will register a huge, potentially disastrous, loss in income. It is against this silencing and self-censorship that *Devil on the Cross* makes its bold and strident move: not so much forcing capitalism to confess the truth as (having created a narrative space in which it might do so in a more or less plausible fashion) allowing it to strip itself bare in public, and to condemn itself out of its own mouth in the excess of its arrogance and conceit.

Another form of power which is present throughout the novel, and against which the text tries to break down silence, is the power of patriarchy, especially in its sexually predatory mode. Wariinga's story of sexual exploitation and betrayal is presented as something repeated thousands of times over across the country, and the sources and forms of resistance to this social phenomenon are less well developed and defined than those in opposition to capitalism. Although men in general are exploiters, it is the rich who behave the worst (in a way which threatens to elide class oppression and gender oppression, as some feminists have argued). There are non-exploitative men – Muturi, the student leader, and possibly Gatuiria – but as Wariinga tells the latter (who is complaining about how foreigners exploit African women):

> The foreigners are not entirely to blame ... Even you, the Kenyan men, think that there is no job a woman can do other than cooking your food and massaging your bodies ... A song of praise begins at home. If you Kenyan men were not so scornful and oppressive, the foreigners you talk about so much would not be so contemptuous of us. (245)

As in *Petals of Blood*, the sexual exploitation of the central female character is dramatically avenged, and Wariinga's action – which is in part a rejection of another even more materially advantageous temptation – is as emphatic as resistance can be. The feeling remains, however, that, with her awakened political consciousness, she kills her father in law-to-be, who is also the Rich Old Man who seduced her, as much because he is a leading capitalist exploiter of his people as because he is an unrepentant patriarchal exploiter of vulnerable young women.

Amidst all the analysis of class- and gender-based forms of power, there is still the power of the transformed and transformative individual, reflecting an awareness on Ngugi's part that 'the masses' are not in fact an inchoate mass, that they are composed of individuals uniting in struggle. In this perspective, characters like Gatuiria and especially Wariinga are affected by significant events (the feast) and significant individuals (Muturi, for instance), and they in turn can have an effect on other events or individuals. The transformation of Gatuiria may be less thorough-going than that of Wariinga, but his ability to affect others through his music may be as far-reaching in its consequences as her solitary act of revolutionary justice (even though his final vacillation and inability to side with Wariinga suggests the limitations of his type of culturalist stance).

In fact Gatuiria is the latest embodiment of a continuing problem for the post-colonial nation (and for Ngugi) – the relation of intellectuals to power, and their ability to take relevant political action. Although Ngugi received international support from intellectuals (and others) when he was imprisoned, the failure of Kenyan academics and intellectuals to challenge manifest injustice is something of which he is critical. Worse than that, in Ngugi's eyes, is the hypocrisy of would-be radical intellectuals:

> In fact, the most interesting attack on me did not emanate from Charles Njonjo [former Kenyan attorney-general] … but from petty (sic) bourgeois intellectuals at the university who hide ethnic chauvinism and their mortal terror of progressive class politics behind masks of abstract super-nationalism, and bury their own inaction behind mugs of beer and empty intellectualism about conditions being not yet ripe for action. But at the same time they are scared of openly attacking peasants and workers. So they talk progressive and act conservative; they wear populist intellectual masks in order to better attack any concrete cases of worker-peasant anti-imperialist struggles.[21]

While the student leader who saves Wariinga at the beginning of the novel and is later arrested with Muturi after the attack on the capitalists represents the ability to act, Gatuiria embodies classic intellectual indecision and inertia. The events of the feast do, however, prompt some critical self-reflection:

> We, the intellectuals among the workers, whose side are we on? Are we on the side of the producers or the side of those who live on the products of others? Are we on the side of the workers and peasants or on the side of the

exploiters? Or are we like the hyena which tried to walk
along two different roads at the same time? (205)

The vacillation of intellectuals is one reason why Muturi decides
to trust Wariinga rather than Gatuiria with the gun taken from
the fleeing capitalist. The decision is correct, because although at
the level of his cultural production – his music – Gatuiria sides
more clearly with the people henceforth, when like the proverb-
ial hyena he needs to choose his road decisively (Wariinga or his
family) he remains frozen in inaction.[22]

Gatuiria also embodies part of Fanon's famous schema of
the development of the colonised intellectual. In the chapter 'On
National Culture' in *The Wretched of the Earth*, Fanon highlights three phases which decolonising intellectuals need to pass
through: the assimilated, the worried, and the combative. 'In the
first phase,' Fanon says, 'the native intellectual gives proof that
he has assimilated the culture of the occupying power.'[23] The
product of Western-style education in Kenya and the real thing
for fifteen years in the United States, Gatuiria has certainly had
his assimilated phase – he does not know about his country or
culture; he has difficulty speaking his own language correctly or
without the intrusion of English words and phrases (always a
touchstone of alienation for Ngugi). Gatuiria passes through the
'disturbed' phase of cultural remembering and rediscovery (this
is the journey he is engaged on when we meet him in the novel)
to something like the third or fighting phase where 'the native,
after having tried to lose himself in the people and with the
people, will on the contrary shake the people. Instead of according the people's lethargy an honoured place in his esteem, he
turns himself into an awakener of the people.'[24] It is 'something
like', however, because although Gatuiria hopes that his national
oratorio will 'awaken' the people, to the extent of rousing them
to anger at capitalist exploitation, and above all, inspiring a love
of Kenya, in some ways he has already been left behind by the
political development of the people. The image which Ngugi
gives is that the people are no longer 'lethargic' or sleeping;
politically, their awakened activism has carried them beyond the
culturalism of Gatuiria and his oratorio. Although Gatuiria has

tried to make his music as authentically national as possible, there is still the problem identified by Fanon that 'the native intellectual who comes back to his people by way of cultural achievements behaves in fact like a foreigner.'[25] Gatuiria's failure can be seen as a systemic problem, rather than an individual one, however, attributable to the fact that the Western-style education to which so many post-colonial nations cling fundamentally disables their intellectuals – 'the kind of education bequeathed to us by the whites has clipped the wings of our abilities, leaving us limping like wounded birds' (63) – and it is against this condition that Ngugi's famous strategy of 'decolonising the mind' is aimed.

At the same time, we need to recognise the importance of Gatuiria's desire to create a genuinely national cultural artefact (and a politicised one), not least because it represents a kind of parallel to what Ngugi is attempting with the novel itself. A further question to consider is the extent to which each can be regarded as genuinely popular (in the sense of reflecting or being rooted in the lives and culture of the people, not in the sense of being commercially successful). Gatuiria's efforts to encapsulate pre-colonial, colonial and post-colonial moments offers parallels with Ngugi's oeuvre, but the fact that he remains committed to the production of an 'oratorio' suggests a continuing investment in Western genres which Ngugi is doing more to break free of.

Although a number of continuities with earlier works were mentioned at the beginning of the chapter, *Devil on the Cross* represents a significant shift, with all kinds of boundaries blurred or transgressed. One example is the boundary between novelistic realism and what lies beyond: fantasy, the supernatural, magic realism, the hyper-real, Bakhtinian grotesque realism, etc. This is blurred from the beginning of the novel, with the presentation of the text as a mystical vision, the result of prayer, fasting and revelation (but none the less real for all that) of the Gicaandi Player, who is also the Prophet of Justice, and with the opening words of his narrative: 'The Devil appeared to Jacinta Wariinga one Sunday on a golf course …'

(10), both of which elements foreground questions of visions and 'voices', of belief and fact, and of the limits of prosaic reality. By and large, the two registers of the real and the fantastic belong to two different worlds in *Devil on the Cross*: the latter to the cave which is the den of the capitalist 'thieves and robbers'; the former to the world outside, but the fantastic is not contained within the cave and constantly leaks into the everyday reality of the characters, especially Wariinga. This is underlined in the way in which characters find events, especially those in the cave, literally incredible, which on one level they are. The idea that capitalists would boast publicly of the appalling methods they use to exploit, cheat and oppress people in the pursuit of ever-greater profit – which is what the procession of increasingly grotesque and repulsive individuals who want to be crowned 'king of thieves and robbers' do – is hardly believable. At the same time, they are perhaps doing no more than any company which flaunts the half-yearly profit level which is the tangible sign of its corporate success in the extraction of surplus value from its operations. Ngugi presents the 'logical' extension of the capitalist method, and the nightmarish unreality which is its most abiding truth.

The tension and oscillation between things which are unbelievable and at the same time absolutely true pervades the text. The climax of the visions of exploitation is Kimeendeeri's scheme, revealed to Wariinga in her satanic visitation on the golf course, for siphoning off the blood, sweat and energy of the brainwashed workforce – at one and the same time, a pure, dystopian, nightmare future and the literal expression of what capitalism already does. The 'logical extension' approach leads for instance to Nditika wa Nguunji extrapolating from the development of transplant surgery to the possibility of immortality via endless organ replacements – with the enhanced pleasure of extra transplanted penises en route (though unsurprisingly his wife is not to be allowed the same possibility of multi-organic, multi-orgasmic delight).

Questions of divine existence and satanic visitation are debated: 'What I'm saying is that it doesn't matter if the Devil actually exists or if he's merely a certain image of the world' (132) (Gatuiria). '"Don't worry," Wangari said, "those things no longer exist – ogres, killers and eaters of men, bad and good spirits, the Devil with seven horns. All those are mere inventions"' (69). 'Now I can tell you that I know of no devil worse than the employer for whom I have been working' (72) (Muturi). 'I believe God and Satan are images in our brains as we struggle with nature in general, and with human nature in particular' (57) (Muturi). The fact that such rationalisations of the supernatural are presented by important and valorised characters would suggest they are the text's preferred explanation. However, having, as it were, painstakingly constructed the boundaries of the real and the rational in this way, the text then goes on to blur and to undermine them: there is, for example, no way in which Wariinga could realistically or rationally have obtained the information which she gets from the Devil during her discussion with him on the golf course.

The use of the fabular, the grotesque and the supernatural is part of Ngugi's deployment of popular and traditional elements of African culture. Others include poetry, music and song. Ngugi had made use of songs in earlier novels to counterpoint action or instantiate particular traditional practices, but here their extensive use clearly has wider significance in reflecting the different groups in society – even capitalists have their own songs (including perverse use of Christian hymns). Most prominent, though, are the songs of resistance, including Mau Mau songs, sometimes adapted for present circumstances. Maina wa Kinyatti had recently published *Thunder from the Mountain*, a collection of Mau Mau songs which proved highly contentious with the Kenyan ruling class and with certain historians: 'The radical utilisation of an earlier generation's sentiments has demanded their ideological refinement, if clumsy Marxification can be so called.'[26] Ngugi, 'clumsy Marxification' notwithstanding, regards Kinyatti's book as a milestone, and is concerned both to promote the Mau Mau songs as important popular cultural texts and to retain the memory of what the struggle meant.

Even more numerous than the songs in the novel are the proverbs, some of which, 'too much haste splits the bean', 'a rich man's fart has no smell', recur frequently. The latter is significant not only because of the insight it offers into the effect of money and class in society, but also because of its highlighting of what, following Bakhtin, we might call the 'lower bodily strata'. If Carole Sicherman's categorisation of the Gikuyu as 'body-shy people' is correct, then the frequent appearances of grotesque or obscene bodies or bodily references in *Devil on the Cross* must make it all the more shocking a text for its target audience (unless Sicherman is talking about actual physical bodies and not references to them or descriptions of them).[27]

This oppositional use of the grotesque body (since very often it is society's Others – the poor, those of different ethnicity, the sexually 'deviant' – who are categorised by the dominant group as grotesque) relates to Bakhtin's discussion of carnival and the scatological as a site of resistance by the people to their rulers, resistance which could take a variety of forms:

> On the negative, critical side, the carnivalesque suggests a demystificatory instrument for everything in the social formation which renders such collectivity difficult of access: class hierarchy, political manipulation, sexual repression, dogmatism and paranoia.[28]

and such a perspective clearly has much in common with what Ngugi is aiming to do in *Devil on the Cross* in terms of criticising oppression and promoting a united opposition.

The standard Bakhtinian obverse of the grotesque body would be the classical, and in *Devil on the Cross* Wariinga takes that role, but instead of the sanitised, desexualised form which the classical body typically takes, Wariinga incarnates classical (but not simply traditional) African beauty, her increasing assumption of which is both an act of self-affirmation and a rejection of the neo-colonial ideologies of female beauty which had previously so oppressed her and which lead many African women into self-mutilation with skin lightening and hair straightening. The fact that Wariinga performs this role of oppositional class/national embodiment in the novel offers a possible redemptive reading for the fact that the text 'gazes' at her in ways which might otherwise appear unacceptably object-ifying and voyeuristic.

Song, poetry, music: not only do these stress *Devil on the Cross*'s links with African popular culture in general, and orature in particular, they also mark it as an entirely different type of novel – one to be performed. As Ngugi has remarked on a number of occasions, texts in Gikuyu would be read in the evening to family and friends; they would therefore already be turned into something far removed from the typical silent and solitary consumption of the Western novel, but the construction of *Devil on the Cross* seems to require something altogether more performative. This in turn can be seen as related to its presentation as *gicaandi*:

> Even a cursory reading of a *gicaandi* text reveals the complex interplay of genres – riddles, proverbs, biograph-ical 'information', historical commentary – and a perform-ative dramatic quality which invests in voice, gesture and attention to the audience. As an event that takes place in the public square, *gicaandi* is not only a performance text but a site of performance, providing a model for interpersonal and public discourse.[29]

Gicaandi also offers one of Ngugi's encapsulations of the relation of author or performer and audience, which is simul-taneously one of the ways in which the text tackles the relation of individual and collective. Despite his reluctance to tell such a shameful story, the Gicaandi Player is persuaded by 'many voices' urging him to speak, as well as the voice 'like a great clap of thunder' telling him that his prophecy is not to be kept to himself, and, ultimately, the realisation that 'the voice of the people is the voice of God'. (Presumably the '*vox populi, vox dei*' realisation retrospectively legitimates or rationalises the thun-derous voice, which might otherwise be altogether more problematic, in view of the way in which 'voices' operate in the novel.) The relation of author/performer and audience, figured within the text in their different ways by Gatuiria and the Gicaandi Player, is one with which Ngugi continues to wrestle.

A final aspect of *Devil on the Cross* which draws together issues of audience, address, the popular, education, cultural authenticity, hegemony, textual politics, anti-imperialism and the role of intellectuals, is the language question. This, for better or worse, is the one theoretical issue above all others with which Ngugi's name is now associated worldwide; better, in that it has focused a great deal of attention on the subject; worse, in that the argument tends to repeat the same limited positions and perspectives, and also because the complexity of Ngugi's cultural politics becomes reduced to this one issue. It is the language question above all which gets Ngugi noticed by post-colonial theorists like Said and Spivak, and Spivak notes (without in any way endorsing) the view that 'when Ngugi decided to write in Kikuyu, some thought he was bringing a private language into the public sphere.'[30] (It is perhaps worth noting in passing that Spivak, generally so punctilious on questions of proper usage – and Eurocentric error – should write 'Kikuyu', the mark of a historical error perpetrated by colonialists who could not get to grips with the initial consonantal sound in Gikuyu.) The question of post-colonial writers' choice of language is frequently reduced to: 'write in English and operate on the world stage' versus 'write in the language of the coloniser and continue to serve their interests', or to: 'write in your native language and condemn yourself to obscurity' versus 'write in your own language and speak at last to your own people'. While Ngugi would no doubt broadly agree with the second proposition in each of these pairs, there is rather more to his position than that. Certainly he is unhappy with the ease with which many writers simply accept the inevitability of using a colonial language – what Achebe called 'the fatalistic logic of the unassailable position of English in our literature', which in itself represents a significant revision of his earlier and more widely-known statements, such as 'I have been given the English language and I intend to use it.'

Decolonising the Mind is Ngugi's most famous and

extensive engagement with the language question, something which has concerned him since his student days at Leeds, and which has its practical roots in the moves to abolish the English Department at the University of Nairobi. He had been writing and speaking on the topic since the seventies, and, more importantly, had begun practising it before his detention in the co-authored, co-operatively produced play *Ngaahika Ndeenda*. It was the popular activist implications of this project which led to his arrest. Up to that point, he had not used Gikuyu in his fiction, but in *Detained* he chronicles the emergence of the new project:

> I had resolved to use a language which did not have a modern novel, a challenge to myself, and a way of affirming my faith in the possibilities of the languages of all the different Kenyan nationalities, languages whose development as vehicles for the Kenyan people's anti-imperialist struggles had been actively suppressed by the British colonial regime (1895–1963) and by the neo-colonial regime of Kenyatta and his comprador KANU cohorts.[31]

From this complex act of literary experimentation, cultural reaffirmation and historical recuperation emerges *Devil on the Cross*. As Ngugi came to realise, resistance at the level of language is far from being a merely symbolic matter: 'The domination of a people's language by the languages of the colonising nations was crucial to the domination of the mental universe of the colonised.'[32] In turn Ngugi regards this sphere of mental control as the most important area of colonial domination.

For Ngugi, the practical experience of the Kamiriithu theatre project changed his outlook on language and cultural production generally. Shortly before that, he had started writing in English a story with a Faustian theme, called *Devil on the Cross*, but abandoned it when *Ngaahika Ndeenda* was being written. After Kamiriithu, and in prison, the text was both re-thought and linguistically transposed, becoming *Caitaani Mutharaba'ini*. As Ngugi has pointed out, his decision meant grappling with a language whose colonial legacy of reduction to written form by non-native speakers (in the shape of missionary efforts to produce a written form suitable for Bibles) left it marked with a fundamental instability (Europeans could not properly distinguish the long and short vowels so crucial to meaning in Gikuyu) which Ngugi could try to resolve only via strict control of meaning through context.

Initially unsure how far his use of Gikuyu would necessitate a different kind of novel, Ngugi was nevertheless concerned to bring writing closer to ordinary people in terms of the inclusion of elements of orature as well as a clearer plot line, a stronger story element, and above all a content which was relevant, 'which had the weight and complexity and the challenge of their everyday struggles'.[33] His success in this is indicated by the speed with which *Caitaani Mutharaba'ini* became a Kenyan bestseller – the first print run selling out within a month, rather than the original estimate of three to five years – in a country where levels of literacy and disposable income militate strongly against such an occurrence. Importantly for Ngugi, the book was appropriated into the oral tradition, especially in terms of communal consumption, and was read to family groups, to workers during lunchbreaks, and to people in bars.

The production of a culturally relevant text is significant at the national level, but its importance does not stop there. In a very Fanonian manner, Ngugi stresses the extent to which, for progressive intellectuals and others, 'the quest for relevance is not a call for isolationism but a recognition that national liberation is the basis of an internationalism of all the democratic and social struggles for human equality, peace and justice.'[34] The globalising of struggle is not the only move beyond the national, however: even at the stage of the Nairobi literature debate, Ngugi and his colleagues envisaged widening spheres of (relevant) study – national literature; regional literature; African literature; Black texts in the diaspora; and so on – and part of that process is the ability of national literatures to speak to one another more readily, and not in the languages of the colonisers. *Caitaani Mutharaba'ini*'s early translation into Kiswahili is for Ngugi an important dimension of this. For Ngugi, the point of the use of a national language – however small its constituency – is to give it its proper place as a major component in the construction of national identity, as the vehicle for national cultural production, and as a visible and valued linguistic form in its own right. That applies as much to 'nations' such as the Gikuyu, Luo or Masai who only make up part of the Kenyan nation-state as it does to more linguistically or culturally homogenous national formations.

Perhaps the single most important aspect of the language question is that the choice of an indigenous language opens the way to participant, democratic, politicised cultural production, reminiscent of Brecht's work in the theatre in the 1930s (indeed, the theatre is perhaps the most fruitful area for this type of work), and approaches the ideal for someone with Ngugi's politics. 'Opens the way' is the operative phrase, however, as Ngugi is aware: 'But writing in our languages per se – although a necessary first step in the correct direction – will not itself bring about the renaissance in African cultures if that literature does not carry the content of our people's anti-imperialist struggles to liberate their productive forces from foreign control.'[35]

As Ngugi has commented on many occasions, the experience of Kamiriithu changed his life, and while the experience is perhaps more important than the texts associated with it, it is still worth pausing over *Ngaahika Ndeenda* (translated as *I Will Marry When I Want*) since it, even more than *Devil on the Cross*, embodies something like an approximation of Ngugi's ideal text. Certainly, from what he has said about it, it would be hard to imagine a more culturally or linguistically accurate text, or a more democratically interactive one, since all rehearsals were held in public and villagers of all ages and backgrounds at Kamiriithu commented on, and corrected, the accuracy of the authors' representation of the language and actions of the characters (as appropriate for someone of that age and social location), as well as the performing of songs, dances and ceremonies – and sometimes became performers themselves on that basis. Both the authors and the villagers declared that the process of organising the play had been profoundly educational.

The strenuous efforts of the Kenyan authorities to put obstacles in the way of *Ngaahika Ndeenda* and its successor *Maitu Njugira* (translated as *Mother, Sing For Me*); the decision to ban the latter and destroy the Kamiriithu Community Centre; the arrest and subsequent harassment of Ngugi, and his choice of exile rather than face re-arrest – all of these indicate clearly the danger which any raising of the political consciousness of ordinary people represents to neo-colonial governments. As Gicaamba says, the prayer of the ruling class is: 'Oh God in Heaven / Shut the eyes of the poor / The workers and the peasants / The masses as a whole / Ensure that they never wake up and open their eyes / To see what we are really doing to them.'[36]

I Will Marry When I Want is set in the present, but instantiates the active remembering of the past, from historical events to cultural practices. It also shows how the actions and processes of the past can return, their apparent 'pastness' no guarantee either of non-repetition or, following Marx's famous formulation, that any such repetition will take the form of farce rather than tragedy. The story is the all-too-familiar one of the ordinary people's loss of land, but the context and methods are entirely post-colonial: the expropriators are the black middle class rather than the white colonialists; the peasants have legal rights to the land enshrined in title deeds; the methods of expropriation are bank loans and debts rather than simple *force majeure*; the results, however, are the same. Or almost: despite the blatant and apparently irreversible theft of Kiguunda's land by his employer Ahab Kioi, Ngugi ends the play with both an analysis of the problems of Kiguunda by his thoughtful worker friend Gicaamba, and a stirring song calling for unity and organisation among workers and peasants and prophesying the imminent uprising of the oppressed. (Whether it was the mere fact of such calls to arms addressed to the masses which so disturbed the Kenyan ruling class, or that they were being issued in a language which the masses could actually understand, Ngugi's activist populism was too much for them to bear.)

The play relates to issues of exploitation and examines the range of forms which it can take – class (Kiguunda by Kioi), sexual (Kiguunda's daughter Gathoni by Kioi's son John Muhuuni) and religious, offering an extensive and bitter critique of the religious hypocrisy and opportunism of the post-colonial ruling class, as well as the way in which Christianity can continue to be at best an intrusive (neo) colonial irrelevance for ordinary people, and at worst a means of their active oppression. The action of the play is punctuated and commented upon by (as well as in some respects structured around – if not actually subordinated to) songs of all kinds. Different groups and individuals have different types of song, and most importantly, there is a sense of song being an integral part of the process of people's production of self-understanding, rather than a jolly alternative to action, as in musical productions from Hollywood to Bollywood. It represents both the popular (in terms of appeal and accessibility) and activist (having been – and continuing to be – important in political mobilisation, as Mau Mau demonstrated so forcibly) and both of these are aspects which Ngugi is concerned to retain in the rather different format of his most recent novel, *Matigari*.

Matigari

Matigari is Ngugi's novel from exile, the first and so far the only novel written since he was forced into possibly permanent exile by the certainty of re-arrest if he returned to Kenya. That certainty has made of him an exemplar of one of the figures taken as typifying the post-colonial world – the intellectual as exile. Although in *Representations of the Intellectual* Said says that 'exile is one of the saddest fates', he does go on to point out a range of advantages:

> What Adorno doesn't speak about are indeed the pleasures of exile, those different arrangements of living and eccentric angles of vision that it can sometimes afford which enliven the intellectual's vocation, without perhaps alleviating every last anxiety or feeling of bitter solitude.[37]

In his most recent writing, such as the preface to the re-issued and reworked *Writers in Politics,* Ngugi for the first time briefly alludes to something positive in his experience of exile, in this case the 'exhilaration' at being able to teach political ideas without the fear of imprisonment. Beyond that, there is little indication that he believes in the Saidian pleasures of exile – indeed, there is an important sense in which he did not need exile in order to achieve that state which, in Said's view, is a particularly productive effect of the shock and dislocation of exile:

> A second advantage to what in effect is the exile stand-point for the intellectual is that you tend to see things not as they are, but as they have come to be that way. Look at the situations as contingent not as inevitable, look at them as the results of a series of historical choices made by men and women, as facts of society made by human beings and not as natural or god-given, therefore unchangeable, permanent, irreversible.[38]

While such a perspective might be insufficiently developed among intellectuals in general, and those in the West in particular, it is obviously one which Ngugi has held for years – indeed it was precisely such a perspective which inspired the activities which led to his arrest and exile.

The combination of prison and exile represents for Ngugi a very common fate for African writers, and in *Moving the Centre* he ponders the connection between the two:

> In both cases the writer is heavily aware of his loss of freedom. He is haunted by a tremendous longing for a connection. Exile can be even worse than prison. Some people have been known to survive prison in their own countries better than 'freedom' in physical exile.[39]

In addition to the largely or wholly voluntary kinds of exile (such as that of the Negritude writers in France), and the coerced (himself, or Alex La Guma and Lewis Nkosi from South Africa), Ngugi identifies another form which is more pervasive, perhaps more metaphorical, but no less pernicious for all that. In this perspective, the combined effects of Western-style education for intellectuals in general, and the choice of writing in Western languages for writers like Ngugi, alienate or exile the educated elite from their own people. However, just as the social fact of prostitution functions in the novels as a metaphor for conditions affecting the whole country or even the whole continent, so exile represents a problem which concerns the whole of Africa:

> The situation of the writer in twentieth-century Africa mirrors that of the larger society. For if the writer has been in a state of exile – whether it is physical or spiritual – the people themselves have been in exile in relation to their economic and political landscape … Africa is a continent alienated from itself by years of alien conquests and internal despots. Thus the state of exile in the literary landscape reflects a larger state of alienation in the society as a whole.[40]

A broadened or more metaphorical application of the idea of exile is something which Ngugi shares with Said, though his metaphorical use of exile as (negative) cultural or economic alienation can seem a long way from Said's (largely beneficial) exile as critical distance from an unacceptable institution or political system. Said does, however, acknowledge that actual exile is not an indispensable precondition for the production of the kind of critical stance he is advocating, and that within the boundaries of their nations, intellectuals can be divided into 'yea-sayers' and 'nay-sayers' (which inevitably recalls Ngugi's discussion in *Detained* of Kenyan leaders or intellectuals who, in his words, said yes or no to colonialism). The 'nay-sayers' are independent, oppositional, critical, alienated or 'exiled' from a system or society which they cannot accept. Once again, criticism from within was obviously Ngugi's stance for a number of years prior to having to leave Kenya.

The idea of the individual profoundly at odds with what their own society has become, or critical of its power relations, applies very strongly to Matigari. Although as a former chauffeur and plantation worker he is as far removed from 'typical' intellectuals like Gatuiria as any of Ngugi's central characters, he does nevertheless provide a good example of Gramsci's organic intellectual. Organic intellectuals are the thinkers, writers and organisers which any social class produces, and who, particularly in the case of the working class, do not have to have had much or any formal education. They are ideologically and politically affiliated to that class, unlike those individuals, products of the educational system, who are 'won over' to the side of the ruling class or some other powerful group – which is obviously an acute problem in neo-colonial circumstances. Matigari's awareness of the problems of society derives from a combination of indigenous (especially class-based) knowledge, enshrined for example in proverbs, and his own life experiences. His estranged/outsider's perspective is the product of his political position but also of the distance created by his years of life in the forest, unaware of the changes occurring in society at large. In a perfect example of the process of reciprocal education and consciousness-raising which typifies the 'pedagogy of the oppressed' and the production of organic intellectuals, when Matigari and the militant worker Ngaruro wa Kirira are locked up in mental hospital, they spend their time discussing ideas and analysing political groups and strategies.[41] They both instantiate the powerful combining of theory and praxis which is the ultimate aim of Marxism and which contrasts them so forcefully with most of the other 'intellectuals' in the novel.

As Matigari journeys in search of truth and justice, he visits representative intellectuals – the student, the teacher, the priest – and experiences different forms of betrayal. While the first two have – very disappointingly for Matigari – gone back on their former more radical utterances through fear of the consequences, the latter, who represents *the* traditional intellectual, historically allied with the ruling class, is understandably less inclined to assist Matigari in his 'subversive' quest, even though his refusal to help Matigari – and through him .Guthera – arguably constitutes the greatest betrayal of responsibility. (There is an additional sense in which Matigari's quest for truth and justice aligns him with 'proper' intellectuals: the French thinker Julien Benda, for example, felt that it was the duty of intellectuals to set up an organisation 'whose sole cult was justice and truth'.[42])

In the trial scene which crowns the Minister for Truth and Justice's visit, the Permanent Professor of the History of Parrotology, the Ph.D. in Parrotology, and the editor of *Daily Parrotry* typify those intellectuals who have sold their souls to His Excellency Ole Excellence's oppressive regime. Given what we have already seen of those forms of intellectual betrayal which anger Ngugi, and remembering the arguments over historical fact and interpretation examined in the context of *Petals of Blood*, it is no surprise that one of the regime's mouthpieces should be a professor of history, especially when he and others like him produce accounts of history which blatantly serve the interests of the regime, such as the conclusion of their recent conference: 'Those who joined hands with the colonialists in protecting the law – *loyalists* – are really the ones who made the colonialists give us independence on a platter' (103). This, in the society to which Matigari has returned, is 'dispassionate' knowledge, formulated 'without the kind of *distortion* you find with some of those *fiction* writers' (103). On one level, the 'parrotology' episode partakes of the same broad humour as the feast in *Devil on the Cross* with its reliance on sometimes grotesque exaggeration. On another level, it is – incredibly – the literal truth of Daniel Arap Moi's view of proper politics in contemporary Kenya. In a speech in September 1984 (while Ngugi was writing the novel) Moi called on 'ministers, assistant ministers, and every other person to sing like parrots' in faithfully echoing his political position, and doing exactly what he said.[43] Unswerving 'Nyayoism' (or Follow in My Footsteps) as Moi calls his political 'philosophy', is, he believes, the only permissible political behaviour.

The fact of Matigari's critical or oppositional distance from his society is deeply ironic, given that this novel is the most powerful example of a theme which runs all through Ngugi's writings, namely that of return, and the fundamental desire of return is obviously the abolition of distance. At the beginning of the novel, Matigari the freedom fighter returns after years of armed struggle in his country's forests, having finally defeated his long-time enemy, the colonialist Settler Williams. Burying his weapons, he puts on 'a belt of peace' and sets out to recover his home and reunite his scattered family, but thenceforward, things do not go at all as he had planned. Insofar as Matigari represents an individual character, his return includes the poignancy of his search for his family, after such a long absence, and the desire that they all re-enter their house together. Insofar as he is a collective character, he embodies different 'returns': the re-forming or re-creation of certain kinds of social groupings or alliances – the 'family', etc. – in the contemporary situation; the return home of a generation of freedom fighters, since the struggle is apparently over; or alternatively, the fighters' return in the sense of their re-emergence, precisely because the struggle is not over, since the conditions for which it was waged have not been delivered – and indeed the current neo-colonial dispensation is in some ways far worse than colonialism. There is also the sense in which he embodies the need to return to armed resistance, peaceful means having failed; and in the words of the title of one of Ngugi's essays in *Barrel of a Pen*, 'Mau Mau is coming back'.[44] At the mythic level, which is neither precisely individual nor collective in these terms, Matigari evokes a very different kind of return – the Second Coming of Christ – a possibility vehemently denied by the regime. There is further irony in Matigari's return in that he believes his period of exile or separation from home and family is at an end, when in fact he is about to begin a period of deeper exile and alienation from his brutal and materialist society. (At the same time, to the extent that he recovers family and community in the shape of Guthera and Muriuki, his exile *is* at an end.)

These uncertain or contradictory meanings are very much the result of the multiple meanings embodied in Matigari himself. In the words of the question which runs throughout the book, 'Who was Matigari ma Njiruungi?' At the very least, he is simultaneously an individual freedom fighter and all those who never gave up the struggle for true independence. He is also the archetypal questing hero of myth and folktale, and in the introductory 'Notes on the English Edition', Ngugi provides one origin for him in the Kenyan story of the search for Old Man Ndiiro. He has clear links with Jesus, and with superhuman heroes of both African and Western narratives. However, as Ann Biersteker says:

> 'Matigari' is, or is to some readers, Jesus, General Stanley Mathenge, Elijah Masinde, Superman, the Terminator, and Ngugi writing as prophet. Karl Marx, Frantz Fanon, and Dedan Kimathi might also be suggested. Bertolt Brecht, Shaaban Robert, Muyaka bin Haji, Martin Luther King Jr., Abdallatif Abdalla, Gakaara wa Wanjau, and Ngugi writing as socialist and *gicaandu* player are additional possibilities.[45]

The list does not stop there (though no doubt many will feel it should have stopped long since). Despite the clear desire for an allegorical dimension to the novel (and at the same time a lack of precision typical of this text about the nature of the allegorical reference); despite the explicit authorial invitation to the reader to locate the narrative in the time and place of their choosing; despite the presence of, for instance, Marxist and Fanonian elements in the text, the idea that Matigari *is* Marx, or Fanon, or Brecht, or the Terminator (or most of the others in the list) can only seem like an impoverishment of what Ngugi is trying to achieve in the novel. It is also interesting that such a list does not contain the one major allegorical reference supplied by Ngugi himself. In an interview with *Third World Quarterly*, he said that 'the character of Matigari can be seen first in a general sense as representing the collective worker in history'[46] and it is notable that all the alternatives in Ann Biersteker's list are significant named individuals rather than anonymous collectivities. As Matigari remarks to Ngaruro, 'a name can have more than one claimant' (24), and the meaning of his own name can change from the individual to the collective in the space of a sentence: 'Your days are numbered! I shall come back tomorrow. We are the patriots who survived: Matigari ma Njiruungi!' (124). As well as the symbol of the worker ('There is no job that these hands of mine have not done for the settler' (143)) Matigari also represents a trans-historical collective presence – the spirit of the nation ('don't you dare touch me, I am as old as this country' (112)) and especially the nation in opposition to foreign incursions ('just consider, I was there at the time of the Portuguese, and at the time of the Arabs, and at the time of the British ...' (45)).

The collective aspect in *Matigari* extends even to the concept of divinity. In the course of his quest, Matigari accumulates a range of Christian and mythic connotations (far more, indeed, than any other character in Ngugi's work). Critics have regarded this as an inability on Ngugi's part to rid himself of that Christian influence which had manifested itself in earlier works. Arguably, however, the Christian elements are included, and built up, precisely in order that they may be 'misused' by being secularised, and transformed in other, 'better', forms of connection or community. Thus, for instance, when Matigari is asked directly whether he is Jesus, and whether this is the Second Coming, he replies at length:

> No ... The God who is prophesied is in you, in me, and in the other humans. He has always been there inside us since the beginning of time. Imperialism has tried to kill that God within us. But one day that God will return from the dead. Yes, one day that God within us will come alive and liberate us who believe in him. (156)

Matigari's vision as he sets it out here is egalitarian, collective and non-transcendent, and thus has little in common with the religious framework into which characters (and critics) try to force it.

The collective dimension is important above all because it gives Matigari's search and struggle the weight both of historical continuity and contemporary relevance. There is also the sense in which it represents one side or the other of the fundamental binary oppositions which structure the novel. Here, 'the people', in the sense of mutual supportiveness and the social, is opposed to neo-colonialism as the rampant individualism generated by capitalism and personified in John Boy Junior:

> *Mzee*, I would ask you to learn the meaning of the word 'individual'. Our country has remained in darkness because

of the ignorance of our people. They don't know the importance of the word 'individual' as opposed to the word 'masses'. White people are advanced because they respect that word, and because they know the *freedom of the individual*, which means the freedom of everyone to follow his own whims without worrying about the others. (48–9)

As Ann Biersteker's list and the range of interpretative options might indicate, *Matigari* is Ngugi's least realist text, or the least concerned with the conventions of novelistic realism. The freedom offered to the reader to determine not only the historical and geographical location but also the duration of the narrative goes well beyond the deliberate imprecisions of allegory into a type of textuality more akin to dream, or a kind of playfulness associated with postmodernism, and certainly numbers of critics want to align *Matigari* with postmodernism despite the theoretical and political problems which that involves. This is particularly the case with critics in the United States, but is also true of Africans. F. Odun Balogun, for instance, feels that '*Matigari* is ... a multivocal postmodernist deconstructionist experiment', though she also says in the same sentence that it is 'a politically satiric and realistic novel'.[47] While it is not immediately clear on what grounds a novel would qualify as realist *and* 'postmodernist deconstructionist', Balogun repeats her belief in its realist qualities:

> *Matigari* is also convincingly constructed as a traditional novel that adheres strictly to all the principles of formal realism as analyzed by Ian Watt in *The Rise of the Novel*. Verisimilitude of character, setting, action and language or style are critical tests of realism, and, in this respect, *Matigari* easily passes in every detail.[48]

For a growing number of post-colonial critics, however, postmodernism, rather than being a culturally liberatory process, appears as just another unhelpful aspect of a dominatory Western (imperialist) culture. Ian Adam and Helen Tiffin, for example, argue in the introduction to *Past the Last Post – Theorizing Post-Colonialism and Postmodernism* that:

the postmodern (in conjunction with post-structuralism [which would include deconstruction]) has exercised and still is exercising a cultural and intellectual hegemony in relation to the post-colonial world and over post-colonial cultural production.[49]

Postmodern or not, there is perhaps a sense in which Ngugi is playing with the reader: just as there are too many precise textual references (to space flight, or nuclear test ban treaties) to allow the narrative to be placed in any period before the present, or anywhere but the post-colonial world, so even the duration is broadly demarcated – three days (hot, cool and hot), corresponding to the three sections of the narrative. Of course Matigari accomplishes far too much in these 'days' for them to be real, but the fluid spatial and temporal parameters of his quest are of little importance compared to its ethical and political content.

The disruption of realism also occurs at the structural level of the narrative, which is more fragmented (thirteen, nineteen and twenty-one subsections respectively) than any other of Ngugi's works. Also, as Ngugi indicated in an interview, the brevity of many of these is the result of his current thinking of textual structure in cinematic terms, as 'shots':

> In my new novel ... I have been influenced by film technique ... I visualize the whole movement of characters as if I was standing behind a camera ... I write as if each scene is captured in a frame, so the whole novel is a series of camera shots.[50]

Remarks such as this are important not simply in terms of understanding the construction of the novel, but also because of the links they inevitably create with Sembene Ousmane, whose politics have so much in common with Ngugi's and who turned to film making for the same reasons Ngugi turned to writing in Gikuyu (and latterly, and tentatively, also to film making).

Matigari is above all a novel of resistance. The very act of writing it is part of Ngugi's opposition to the regime of Arap Moi, and to the neo-colonial conditions which it both exemplifies and helps perpetuate. The narrative is a re-examination of different modes or possibilities of resistance, as well as a call for renewed resistance to neo-colonialism (and a prophecy that such resistance will win in the end). The novel's success in unsettling the regime is visible in the now well-known account of how in 1987 the government first tried to arrest an individual called Matigari who, they had heard, was going round the country demanding truth and justice, and how, having discovered their embarrassing mistake, they had to content themselves with banning the book and seizing all available copies. The novel also presents us with an extension of the broad alliance politics developed in *Petals of Blood* and *Devil on the Cross*. As well as the worker and peasant coalition symbolised by Matigari and Ngaruro wa Kibiiro which is fundamental to Ngugi's political perspective, Matigari, Guthera and Muriuki form a 'family' of resistance; importantly, there is also the sense of a generational transfer of resistance, with the destitute children instigating the destruction of their oppressor's property, and, on the final page, Muriuki taking up Matigari's weapons and the struggle that goes with them. The involvement of Guthera alongside Matigari also marks another step in Ngugi's treatment of women characters in his novels. No Wariinga-like superwoman, Guthera is nevertheless seen as an essential part of the struggle for freedom. (She also comes to the realisation of the need to assert her hitherto-denied humanity, and the oppressors have a price to pay in that regard.)

Guthera, like other recent Ngugi heroines, has been prey to sexual exploitation. In her case, her predicament is made more poignant (even bizarre) by the extraordinarily high priority she gives to her principles: she has the chance to save her beloved father's life by having sex with a policeman; she refuses, because of her Christian beliefs, and her father is killed; however, the poverty which follows forces her into prostitution. For her, unlike Wanja and Wariinga, there is no narrative of revenge, just a further sacrifice of her principles: she has sex with a policeman as her part in the plan to release Matigari and the others from prison (though at least she could be said to do it as a freely chosen act in pursuit of an end she believes in). Also, while she foregoes any personalised revenge, she participates to a greater extent than other female characters in the struggle against the system which oppresses them all. Sympathy for the victims of gender oppression seems to be a more powerful emotion for Guthera than anger against the perpetrators of class oppression. When she, Matigari and Muriuki find the supposedly ultra-moral wife of the Minister for Truth and Justice naked in her car with her chauffeur, Guthera, rather than pleasure at the discomfiture of a class enemy and oppressor of ordinary people, feels sorry for the woman who will be beaten by her husband when he finds out what she has done. Guthera also ponders the relation between new-found awareness and acting on it:

> Once a person knows, what does she do about it? Or is knowing just good in itself? Is it enough for me just to say that now I know? I want to do something to change whatever it is that makes people live like animals, espe-cially us women. What can we as women do to change our lives? Or will we continue to follow the paths carved out by men? Aren't we in the majority anyway? Let's go! (140)

However, neither for Guthera, nor for any of the other women in the novel is there any opportunity to implement such a strategy. Progress for women can only be left to the future moment of Muriuki's continuation of the struggle, though it is important in terms of the ideology of the text that Guthera has reached this point. It is symptomatic of the perverted 'truth' of the ruling class that the fact that the wife of the Minister of Truth and Justice owns racehorses can be cited as proof of the saying: 'African people's progress, women's progress' – there being, of course, no discernible progress either for 'the people' in general, or for women in particular in the conditions created by this regime.

The principal forms and relations of power with which Ngugi is concerned in *Matigari* are those which anyone acquainted with his recent work could predict with reasonable confidence. That 'predictability' is in Ngugi's eyes no occasion for apology, nor any reason whatsoever for looking for different subject matter. These are for him fundamental truths about the distribution of power in the (post-colonial) world, and are ultimately matters of life and death. *Matigari* depicts power's ability to coerce and cow, as well as co-opt. In addition to the by-now familiar image of the bourgeoisie, parasitic and predatory, who happily go along with the corruption of the system, we see the way in which the repressive deployment of power silences those who might speak out against it such as the student or the teacher. At the same time, although the regime functions in a more thoroughgoing totalitarian way than anything Ngugi has previously depicted (even colonialism at its height) the novel demonstrates that even totalitarianism can be resisted, particularly by an organised people, and perhaps overcome. The tendency towards a Manichean vision of a simplified struggle of good versus evil is even more pronounced in *Matigari* and the later collections of essays. Unlike Manicheanism, however, here the moral dimension is definitely of secondary importance:

> In terms of social change, the present face of the twentieth century is a product of the struggle between two contending forces. On the one hand, imperialism which saw the elevation not simply of the non-producer but of the parasitic non-producer into the dominant ruling power, not just over people from one country but over several nations, races and countries. On the other has been the social revolution which for the first time in human history sought change and often fought for power on behalf of, and from the standpoint of the producer working peoples.[51]

This is not necessarily Ngugi's most elegant formulation of the confrontation, nor necessarily the most historically accurate. Nevertheless, it represents very clearly his strongly-held conviction that there are two sides (irreconcilable, implacably opposed), and that a choice has to be made between them – a realisation which a number of characters in *Matigari* come to sooner or later.

The continuation of colonial domination into neo-colonialism is embodied in the generational transfer of power from Settler

Williams to his son, while John Boy Junior instantiates the black bourgeoisie's rise to (near) equality – and certainly deep complicity – with their former masters in overseeing the smooth running of the capitalist system and the continued exploitation of the ordinary people. While *Devil on the Cross* was principally concerned with the grotesque, monstrous or exorbitant nature of capitalists, the (literal) refrain of *Matigari* is the expropriation of those who work and produce: 'The builder sleeps in the open / The worker is left empty-handed / The tailor goes naked / And the tiller goes to sleep on an empty stomach' (98). The fact that the real workers lack the very things which their labour produces highlights both the injustice and the illogicality of the workings of capitalism. This functional and fundamental irrationality is mirrored in the ever-increasing absurdity of the claims of the regime (which also reflect those of certain post-colonial African governments):

> The Minister for Truth and Justice has said that this is a workers' government. All workers should disassociate themselves from those who are disrupting industrial peace by demanding increases in wages … His Excellency Ole Excellence has said that this is a people's government … The people do not want opposition parties, as they only cause disorder in the country. (7)

The height of absurdity, which, like the Devil's Feast in *Devil on the Cross*, forms the centrepiece of the novel (though it lacks the extremes of grotesqueness), is provided by the Minister of Truth and Justice's meeting, with its parade of Parrotology, perhaps the most shocking aspect of which is the fact that it is no more than the application of Arap Moi's vision of proper government.

In very obvious ways, the novel foregrounds the question of the nature and location of truth, but it is socially embodied and politicised truth with which it is concerned, not abstract notions. Matigari says to the teacher frightened into silence by the power of the regime: 'There are two kinds of wise ones of the stars [i.e. intellectuals]: those who love the truth and those who sell the truth' (92), and the teacher later manages to take a stand on this, shouting as he is led off to prison: 'I also know that there are two truths. One truth belongs to the oppressor; the other belongs to the oppressed' (121). On such truths, whole social systems are constructed: '"There are two worlds," Matigari said to the teacher. "There is the world of those who accept things as they are, and there is that of those who want to change things"' (91).

This image of struggling and competing truths recalls both Foucault's insight that the ability to make statements which count as true is a function of the power invested in discourses and institutions (including governments), and Bakhtin and Voloshinov's assertion that the meaning (and truth) of words is a continuing site of social and political contestation.[52] Whether or not it is axiomatically the case that 'The truth shall set you free', Matigari is very clear that there are some 'truths' which are infinitely more oppressive than others, and that these currently have the upper hand in his country (and beyond), though he believes their period of ascendancy is almost over. If, as Said says in *Representations of the Intellectual*, 'speaking the truth to power' is the proper function of the intellectual, then Matigari obviously fulfils that role, as he relentlessly seeks to bring truth to bear on the operations of the regime. This, in its inclusion of power in the equation, is a more politicised conception of the function of the intellectual than Benda's which was mentioned earlier in the chapter. However, as Matigari demonstrates, speaking the truth to power is far from being a simple or straightforward exercise. Among other things, there is the danger resulting from power's dislike of being faced with truth, and one reason why Matigari's truth is so unpalatable is because he, as newly-returned freedom fighter, confronts the regime most starkly with the extent of its betrayal of the aims, the ideals and the achievements of the liberation struggle. In their various ways, all the texts in this section of the book and this period of Ngugi's career pose the problem, but none embodies as forcefully as *Matigari* the antitheses involved and the scale of the betrayal. There is also the problem of conceptual complexity: Said says that the basic question for intellectuals is 'how does one speak the truth? What truth? For whom and where?'[53] and awareness of the need to take into consideration the fact that truth can be, indeed *is* contextual rather than absolute, complicates the speaking function of the intellectual.

Beyond such delicate intellectual concerns, however, there is the brute fact of power's ability to construct and enforce whatever it likes as 'truth', and in *Matigari* the ruling order works hard to produce a perverted or inverted reality as the 'true' state of things: '"This world is upside down," Matigari suddenly said. "The robber calls the robbed *robber*. The murderer calls the murdered *murderer*, and the wicked calls the righteous *evil*"' (150). This is symptomatic of the way in which the regime operates. Rational popular demands for social justice are labelled extremist and insane, and land their advocate in a mental hospital; at the same time, the government carries out all manner of arbitrary repression whilst proclaiming that it behaves in a strictly democratic and law-abiding way.

Matigari, as mentioned earlier, has come back wearing a 'belt of peace' and for much of the novel is content to pursue his quest for truth and justice peacefully, accumulating Christ-like parallels on the way and regardless of the violent treatment he sometimes receives. Eventually, however, he realises that in view of the deployment of power he faces, such a strategy is bound to fail:

> It dawned on him that one could not defeat the enemy with arms alone, but one could also not defeat the enemy with words alone. One had to have the right words, but these words had to be strengthened by the force of arms. In the pursuit of truth and justice one had to be armed with armed words. (131)

Although in the end he does not manage to re-arm himself, nevertheless he literally lights the flame of resistance, and sparks off direct physical opposition to the neo-colonial regime which will, we assume, be carried on by Muriuki.

While Matigari, Muriuki and others provide representations of resistance, the text itself can be seen as an extension of Ngugi's own brand of resistant cultural politics, in particular, the attempt to produce a 'novel' which, even more than *Devil on the Cross*, is popular, relevant, accessible, and politicising in respect of its primary (Kenyan) audience. Part of that process is making the narrative even more recognisably African by giving it the form of a traditional fable. The fact that that simultaneously makes it more 'universal', since the pattern of the quest story is present in so many cultures, would no doubt be regarded by Ngugi as a clear vindication of his stance that Africanness is no cultural obstacle. Also, if as Bakhtin says, 'the novel's roots must ultimately be sought in folklore',[54] then we could argue that in *Devil on the Cross* and *Matigari* Ngugi is managing simultaneously to be faithful to the truth of his own inherited culture and to that of the imported literary genre. A different relation between the African and European elements is posited by Simon Gikandi:

> His decision to write in Gikuyu enabled him to reject realism without renouncing it, and to experiment with modernist and post-modernist forms without acknowledging their legitimacy. In short, Ngugi's recourse to Gikuyu oral traditions (especially in *Matigari*) allowed him to accept a hitherto unrecognised affinity between modernist and post-modernist forms and African oral traditions.[55]

This is an interesting suggestion, though it is somewhat undermined by the fact that *Petals of Blood* – which was written before the asserted break with the typical novel – is arguably as modernist as anything written subsequently. It also begs the question of why Ngugi, if he is attempting a particularly radical break with European cultural forms and languages, would want to dally with such thoroughly Western modes as modernism and postmodernism, the extent of whose contamination with the ideologies of imperialism continues to be debated in post-colonial circles.

For Gikandi and the South African critic Lewis Nkosi, Ngugi's turn to the traditional is the outcome of a crisis. Gikandi sees this as a personal one: in his eyes, Ngugi's view of the nature of the novel and its relation to society left him with nowhere to go artistically after *Petals of Blood*. Nkosi also sees the crisis as constituted by a creative deadend, but, unlike Gikandi, regards this as a generalised 'crisis of representation' produced by a continent-wide literary exhaustion:

> Ngugi's gradual relinquishment of realistic representation for the world of fairy tale and day dream may provide us with yet another sign of the crisis afflicting the post-colonial novel in Africa generally, in its attempts over the past three decades to plot the story of corruption and exploitation under the leadership of civilian-military dictatorships.[56]

There is much one could say about these assessments. Here, it is perhaps enough to note a fundamental problem with Gikandi's: he states that Ngugi believes that 'the introduction of new forms [of the novel] *depends on* changes in social conditions or ideology ...'[57] The idea that a writer is only 'allowed' to introduce literary changes when society has changed is an impossibly mechanistic conception, and one which Ngugi does not espouse. (The argument that that social change can lead to more general modifications in cultural forms and processes is an altogether different issue.)

Ngugi's drive to Africanise his cultural output also extends to the mechanisms of publishing. As well as having *Matigari* translated into English by a young Kenyan woman rather than doing it himself, Ngugi stipulated that translations into other languages must be done directly from Gikuyu, rather than, as had happened with *Devil on the Cross*, from the English version. This forces other languages and cultures to enter into direct contact with Gikuyu, thereby acknowledging its existence (even if only as a source of frustration for the translator) and is thus part of the process of achieving recognition for African cultures.

At the level of the practical or popular politics of the text, Ngugi was apparently highly successful before the government clampdown. Anecdotal evidence indicates that the book was read aloud and discussed in family groups and workplaces, in buses and in bars, where, by stopping at dramatic moments, readers ensured a steady supply of liquid reward or encouragement from their audience. Achieving the public performance – and discussion – of a narrative in Gikuyu, addressed to and addressing the problems of that community, couched in popular forms (fable, satire, oral narrative mixed with poetic and musical elements), is perhaps as far as Ngugi might be able to go in escaping the formal and ideological constraints of the traditional European novel, as far as he could go in moving from the individually and silently-consumed novel to the communally-read or performed one, and in following the example of Sembene Ousmane by producing texts which not only speak to the people but which also politicise them. Ousmane's well-documented move from writing novels to directing films, in order to reach as many people as possible simultaneously, to transcend barriers of low levels of literacy (by doing away with the need to read anything) and disposable income (by showing films for free whenever possible), and to provide a forum for the analysis of texts and ideas (audiences are encouraged to stay behind after the screening and discuss what they have seen) is the best known, and potentially the most successful of such radical cultural projects.

It is no surprise that Ousmane regards Ngugi as a comrade, and that the ideas of each should find echoes in the other:

> Ngugi has reminded us that we all come from different corners of the world but have the same roots in Africa. We give expression to different civilisations and situations but we have the same profession and the same objective ... In the whole of Africa since independence, some thirty years ago, the new African bourgeoisie has killed more African intellectuals than did one hundred years of colonialism, or else they have driven them into exile until, intellectually, they are destroyed. This is to let you know that whenever Ngugi takes up a topic, it is his life that is at issue.[58]

In one of his attacks on post-colonial theorising (not least as, in his eyes, an inappropriate hijacking of the term post-colonial) the Indian Marxist critic Aijaz Ahmad is particularly scornful of a remark of Bob Hodge and Vijay Mishra in their article 'What is post(-)colonialism?'.[59] As Ahmad puts it, 'The claim that "post-colonial writers compose under the shadow of death" is simply preposterous, whatever the blanket term "post-colonial writer" might mean.'[60] Although it is probably unfair (or inaccurate) of Ahmad to criticise Hodge and Mishra for this remark since it appears to be a paraphrasing of points from *The Empire Writes Back*, the idea that being a post-colonial writer can involve some greater or smaller risk of death is clearly far from 'preposterous' for post-colonial writers such as Ousmane and Ngugi.[61] Indeed, it is tempting to turn the accusation around and to suggest that it is precisely sweeping dismissals of this kind which are themselves 'preposterous'. Obviously, some parts of the post-colonial world are less dangerous than others, but the notion that being a post-colonial writer is a risk-free profession, especially on home ground, is simply untenable. The recent secret escape of Taslima Nasreen from Bangladesh into exile in the face of repeated death threats is just one of the high profile examples of the price which post-colonial writers and intellectuals pay for following their profession, an issue which Ngugi pursues in his essays, and one to which we shall return in the next chapter.

Essays

ALTHOUGH Ngugi is, quite rightly, regarded as a novelist rather than an essayist, he has now published more books of non-fiction than of fiction. There is an interesting reverse symmetry about his production in these two areas, with the early period heavily weighted towards fiction, and the later towards non-fiction. In the 1960s and 1970s, which saw the publication of four novels, two plays and a collection of short stories, Ngugi produced only one volume of essays. Conversely, since 1987, the year of *Matigari*, Ngugi has published no fiction at all, but the same period has seen three collections of essays, or four if we, along with Ngugi, regard the revised and reissued *Writers in Politics* as a new book. It is also notable how little analysis there has been of the essays, the one exception being *Decolonising the Mind* and especially 'The Language of African Literature', since it is the principal source for Ngugi's arguments regarding the use of indigenous African languages, for which he has almost become more famous than for his novels. This critical neglect of the essays is partly, no doubt, because they are relatively recent, partly because critics tend to treat them as second-level commentary on the important (i.e. literary) texts, and partly because African writers in general have not been regarded as significant essayists. To an extent, this book might seem as if it were perpetuating something of that dominant position, since it accords just one chapter to all the collections of essays, as opposed to one chapter each for the novels. However, the essays themselves are not being studied as mere adjuncts of the important business of fiction production, but like the novels, as examinations of, and interventions in, the field of society, culture and politics in the post-colonial world in general, and Kenya in particular.

Like the novels, but to a greater degree, the essays focus on, and frequently revisit, a range of important themes, or themes which Ngugi considers important, and our necessarily brief overview of them in this chapter will do likewise, giving some indication of the range of topics covered, but concentrating on a few of the most relevant and substantial, and providing a sense of the ways in which they are interwoven across the essays. Among the topics which are revisited, repeated, extended and amended in the course of Ngugi's career are culture, literature, the artist and intellectual, education, language, history, politics, the nation, colonialism, neo-colonialism and imperialism. Ngugi himself recognises the element of repetition, saying in the Introduction to *Decolonising the Mind*: 'For those who have read my books *Homecoming, Writers in Politics, Barrel of a Pen*, and even *Detained: A Writer's Prison Diary*, there may be a feeling of *déjà-vu*. Such a reaction will not be far from the truth.'[1] Arguably, such repetition owes more to a perceived need on Ngugi's part to ensure that certain topics continue to be discussed than to an inability to say something different. Indeed, it would be possible to see Ngugi's stance as one of resistance to the obligation to come up with something new for every one of the many speeches, conference papers, essays and articles that are demanded of him, an obligation which would itself look like the commodification of intellectual work, relentless 'newness' being the defining characteristic of the commodity. In his latest collection, *Penpoints, Gunpoints and Dreams*, Ngugi discusses repetition as a fundamental aspect of traditional African orature, where it is regarded as crucial to the communication of meaning – though that is not to suggest that such an idea has always inspired his own repetitions.

Of Ngugi's central themes, culture is perhaps the most common, *Decolonising the Mind* being the only book in which it does not figure as either a section heading or the title of an individual essay. The earliest, briefest statement on culture, especially national culture, is 'Kenya: the Two Rifts' in *Homecoming*. Here, Ngugi examines the 'vertical rift' caused by ethnicity and tribalism, and the 'horizontal' one caused by class, as well as the absence of a sense of nation resulting from people's excessive concentration on these other – and for Ngugi, extremely limiting – sources of identity formation. As he says, 'to live on the level of race or tribe is to be less than whole.'[2] The attack on tribalism is extended in 'Towards a National Culture', the first essay in the first collection, *Homecoming*, and one which we could reasonably consider as Ngugi's founding statement on the question. Even without the epigraph from *The Wretched of the Earth*, it would be difficult to miss the echoes of, and debt to, Fanon, 'On National Culture' being one of the best-known pieces in Fanon's book. Like its near-namesake, 'Towards a National Culture' examines different perspectives on the past and African culture, and displays a similarly scathing attitude towards those who view the past inappropriately:

> Yet too often ... we talk of African culture as if it were a static commodity which can and should be rescued from the ruins and shrines of yesterday and projected on to a modern stage to be viewed by Africa's children, who, long lost in the labyrinth of foreign paths in an unknown forest, are now thirsty and hungry for the wholesome food of their forefathers. No living culture is ever static.[3]

Another common but inappropriate way of thinking about the African past – and, even more so, present – is via the notion of tribes or tribalism. It is inappropriate for the past because of the extent to which the concept of tribalism was a European imposition, and for the present because even if the existence of 'tribes' in the past is granted, the economic and social circumstances which constituted their existence have vanished, and so it no longer makes sense to think or talk in such terms. The material obsolescence of the tribe and therefore the irrelevance of the concept of tribalism takes us beyond the kind of opposition expressed by Remi in Ngugi's play *The Black Hermit*, where it seems more a question of emotion than economic fact. Rejection of tribalism is something which Ngugi shares with other post-colonial thinkers, and Amilcar Cabral has this to say:

> Today it cannot be said that Africa is tribal. Africa still has remnants of tribalism, in particular as far as the mentality of the people is concerned, but not in the economic structure itself. Moreover, if colonialism, through its action, did anything positive at all, it was precisely to destroy a large part of the existing remnants of tribalism in certain parts of the country.[4]

The fact that tribalism functions only as an ideology rather than a material fact (if one can 'dematerialise' ideology in this way) is paradoxically one reason why it is so potently manipulable by the Arap Moi regime in Kenya, in order to foment division and weaken opposition in the country. Ironically (or logically, Ngugi might argue) that is precisely how colonialism used tribalism.

In the essay 'Church, Culture and Politics' (mentioned in the Contexts and Intertexts chapter) Ngugi argues forcefully that the Christian church in Africa must establish connections with the remnants of traditional African culture in order to begin to undo some of the cultural damage it has caused. At the same time, Ngugi in no way espouses the (nostalgic) nativism of which he has been accused (most frequently in relation to the language debate) which would believe in some sort of cultural resurrection. As he says, 'it is surely not possible to lift tradi-tional structures and cultures intact into modern Africa.'[5]

As well as turning away from the wrong kind of attitude to the past, as for example, Karega does in *Petals of Blood*, there is a need for a correct orientation to the future. Here, Ngugi shares Fanon's belief in the importance of moving political struggle beyond the level of the national, but also states his demand for a socialist future more emphatically than Fanon:

> My thesis, when we come to today's Africa, is very simple: a completely socialised economy, collectively owned and controlled by the people, is necessary for a national culture: a complete and total liberation of the people,

through the elimination of all the exploitative forces, is necessary for a national culture.[6]

In addition, 'Towards a National Culture' contains important embryonic statements of ideas which Ngugi would later examine at greater length, especially in *Decolonising the Mind*, regarding the role of the education system and the centrality of African languages in the production of a national culture, both of them related to his earlier attempt at a radical reform of the English Department in the University of Nairobi.

In the next book, *Writers in Politics*, 'Literature and Society' occupies the strategic position opening the collection, and as with 'Towards a National Culture' it sets out a model of culture, in Raymond Williams' terms, as 'a whole way of life'. Although he uses this broad, inclusive concept, at the same time Ngugi frequently talks of culture in more narrowly-defined ways, separating it from economic and political processes, and seeing it as concerned with questions of communal values and identity: 'A culture, then, embodies a community's structure of values, the basis of their world outlook, and how they see themselves and their place in the universe and in relation to other communities.'[7] Ngugi sees cultural production within particular societies as structured in class terms (dominated by the culture of the ruling class), and between societies as structured by relations such as colonialism (in which context the culture of colonialism is dominant). In each case, the dominant culture tries both to marginalise the dominated culture and to impose itself on the members of the dominated community, working to create a regime which combines hegemonic consent and coercive domination:

> They would like to have a slave who not only accepts that he is a slave, but that he is a slave because he is fated to be nothing else but a slave. Hence he must love and be grateful to the master for his magnanimity in enslaving him to a higher, nobler civilization.[8]

Literature, for Ngugi, is a central element on both sides of the struggle for cultural domination and liberation, and he analyses both the role of Western literature in – wittingly or otherwise – instilling a sense of cultural inferiority in colonised peoples, and that of indigenous literatures in organising resistance to domination. At times, however, his view of the relation between European culture and the colonised can seem extremely mechanistic or determinist – 'the best minds were employed by the European ruling classes for the cultural genocide of the colonised peoples'[9] – which leaves no room for any autonomy on the part of the 'best minds', nor for the sort of resistance which he would otherwise want to claim for African writers and thinkers. Nevertheless, it is not only or always the Europeans who are to blame: the African middle class, as we have seen in Ngugi's novels, functions as their willing accomplices. Ironically, even the unwilling can still end up as accomplices, and some aggressively anti-European positions adopted by writers still serve European dominance. The nativism which in *Home-coming* appeared as simply an unfruitful attitude to the past now seems like a potential screen for the operations of cultural imperialism. As Ngugi says:

> It is important that we understand that cultural imperialism in its era of neo-colonialism is a more danger-ous cancer because it takes new subtle forms and can hide even under the cloak of militant African nationalism, the cry for dead authentic cultural symbolism and other native racist self-assertive banners.[10]

'Literature and Society' also contains what will become one of Ngugi's most consistent points of reference – the fact that colonial control needs to operate at the level of culture as well as politics and the economy in order to be fully effective. (Indeed, the later Ngugi moves from seeing culture as one among many aspects of colonial domination to regarding it as the most important and far-reaching.) This raises the frequently-debated question of the relative weight which should be given to the sphere of culture in this type of analysis. It is true that in the past the role and impact of culture in the functioning of colonialism and imperialism was generally ignored (analyses of imperialism produced by historians or economists unsurprisingly favoured the political or economic dimensions). It is equally true that there is currently a danger of analyses produced by literary critics or cultural theorists overemphasising the importance of culture at the expense of other areas. It is to Ngugi's credit therefore, that however much importance he gives to the cultural sphere, he never loses sight of the economic and political dimensions of imperialism.

While numbers of critics have attacked the allegedly simplistic view of the polarised political battle lines in the modern world in *Matigari*, with its refrain of 'there are two kinds of ...', as a sign of Ngugi's recent aesthetic decline, similar reductivism (or clear-sightedness) appears somewhat earlier in the essays. In 'Kenyan Culture: the National Struggle for Survival', in *Writers in Politics*, Ngugi says 'a central fact of Kenyan life today is the fierce struggle between the cultural forces representing foreign interests and those representing patriotic national interests. This cultural struggle may not always be obvious to a casual observer ...'[11] Although the Western domination of cultural practices (literature, theatre, music) which he examines in the context of Kenya seems far from benign, Ngugi believes that even well-intentioned Western intervention is inappropriate, and that only Kenyans can create a Kenyan culture.

A slightly different perspective on the cultural struggle of the national versus the imperialist occurs in *Barrel of a Pen*, in the essay 'National Identity and Imperialist Domination: the Crisis of Culture in Africa Today', where Ngugi argues that the fight for freedom from external influence is repeatedly falsely posed in terms of tradition versus modernity, conservatism versus progress, or the rural versus the urban. In language which again recalls Fanon in *The Wretched of the Earth*, Ngugi argues for the constructing of national culture as an integral dimension of the fight for autonomy, and as a process which in itself overcomes the false separation of the urban and the rural, the worker and the peasant. The role of ideology in the production of culture is discussed in 'Education for a National Culture', and Ngugi examines the problem that 'in a class-structured society, or in a situation where one nation or race or class is dominated by another, there can never be any neutral education transmitting a neutral culture.'[12] While it is, of course, highly debatable whether a 'neutral' culture could ever exist in the first place, Ngugi's assertion that a situation of political and cultural oppression will fundamentally distort processes of cultural production and transmission is less contentious. In such conditions, where partisanship appears unavoidable, passivity is inconceivable, and Ngugi, echoing Marx's famous 'Theses on Feuerbach', argues that 'Education and culture should not only explain the world but must prepare the recipients to change the world.'[13] That such change needs to proceed in a politically progressive direction perhaps scarcely needs to be mentioned, though it is all the more important, given the role of the colonial and colonially-affiliated education systems in installing and perpetuating Western hegemony in the non-Western world.

The problem of how to liberate culture is the principal organising concept for Ngugi's more recent *Moving the Centre: the Struggle for Cultural Freedom*, and the three sections which comprise the bulk of the collection are entitled, 'Freeing Culture from Eurocentrism', 'Freeing Culture from Colonial Legacies' and 'Freeing Culture from Racism'. One of the important issues here concerns the relations between cultural unity, cultural plurality and universality, and the interaction of the local and the global. Simultaneously acknowledging the existence, and value, of individual or localised cultures and perceiving the possibility, or even emergent actuality, of more generalised forms, is again something which Ngugi shares with Fanon. Negotiating and navigating between terms such as these (as well as their differing connotations) is not always straightforward, and so we find Ngugi stating in 'The Universality of Local Knowledge': 'I am suspicious of the word and the concept of the universal',[14] but also in the Preface to the same collection declaring himself 'an unrepentant universalist'.[15] This, however, is not the result of confusion on Ngugi's part: in the first example he is unhappy about the way in which the West repeatedly turns its own local perspective into the model of the universal; in the second, he is concerned with the universalising liberatory potential of 'true humanism', so called to distinguish it from the covertly racist, falsely universalist Western version of humanism. Difference from, or resistance to, the West (especially in the shape of imperialism) offers another type of universalising process. Ngugi notes the way in which workers all over the world may be employees of, exploited by, and hence in conflict with, the same trans-national corporation (almost inevitably Western-owned): 'In terms of the structures of domination, subordination and resistance, a common global experience is emerging. Gradually a vocabulary of concepts of domination and revolt become part of a shared intellectual tradition.'[16] Curiously, perhaps, the second sentence seems to shift the emphasis from the shared material conditions of exploitation towards the arguably less politically effective realm of intellectual tradition (though it may be the case that Ngugi is aiming to highlight both the concrete experience and the intellectual tradition).

In his most recent collection of essays, *Penpoints, Gunpoints and Dreams*, Ngugi is less interested in culture than in art, though he arguably does not make clear the precise differences he sees between them (which is obviously a problem when using contentious terms such as these). He does, however, retain his basic sense of culture as communal self-production, while giving it some different glosses. In 'Art War With the State', for example, he says: 'In societies that did not have a state, the function of holding things together was carried out by culture.'[17] This is symptomatic of the problems Ngugi gets himself into in his desire to oppose (creative) culture and (coercive) state, since he ignores the way in which state structures could be intimately related to (if not directly expressive of) the specificities of cultures (rather than abstract impositions on them), or conversely the ways in which culture can be coercive (the transgressing of 'cultural' rules can carry severe punishment, including the death penalty, just as much as breaking the laws of the state).

In *Decolonising the Mind*, Ngugi's particular gloss on culture is in the form of 'language as culture'. He says:

> Language as culture is the collective memory bank of a
> people's experience in history. Culture is almost indis-
> tinguishable from the language that makes possible its
> genesis, growth, banking, articulation and indeed its trans-
> mission from one generation to the next.[18]

This prioritising of language is understandable, however, given
Ngugi's aim in *Decolonising the Mind* to set out at length his
position on the role of language in general, and indigenous
African ones in particular, in the cultural sphere. Although
Decolonising the Mind is regarded by many as having sparked
the language debate, even before the book was published, the
issue was being dismissed in some quarters:

> The language question has provoked a fractious, and to
> date intractable, debate … in intellectual circles, it has all
> too often centred around claims of purity and pollution,
> nativism   and   cosmopolitanism,   Eurocentrism   and
> Afrocentrism, rendering an important question into what
> one critic has described as 'a sterile debate'.[19]

The fact that Dieter Riemenschneider's remarks appeared two
years before *Decolonising the Mind* indicates that the debate,
however good or bad, is not simply about Ngugi. While terms
like 'purity and pollution' are obviously strongly value-laden
and emotive, it is not clear why discussion of the others would
necessarily produce 'a sterile debate' (even though it is sometimes hard not to sympathise with the argument that that is
what the debate has in fact become).

In its simplest terms, the debate is about whether African
authors should continue to use the languages of the former
colonial (or currently neo-colonial) powers, or produce works in
their own indigenous languages, and to this extent it is an issue
with potential relevance throughout the post-colonial world.
Beyond this basic position, however, its ramifications are
extensive, and it covers, among others, questions of audience,
address, artistic form, the nature of language itself, publishing,
ethnicity, the relations of nationality and internationality, and
the politics of each and all of these. Its representative positions

are very frequently polarised (hence some of the 'sterility') and personalised, with Achebe taken to stand for those who are determined to continue using European languages, and Ngugi as the high profile advocate of an unequivocal return to indigenous languages.

Although Ngugi has been concerned with the language question for a long time, his position, as he recognises, has not always been progressive or enlightened. As he points out in *Writers in Politics*, in the mid 60s he gave a talk on the advantages of writing in English rather than African languages, citing in justification the extensive vocabulary available to users of English. Despite this (in his terms) early false start, Ngugi has advocated the recognition of the value of African languages since the early 70s at least: 'Equally important for our cultural renaissance is the teaching and study of African languages. We have already seen what any colonial system does: impose its tongue on the subject races and then downgrade the vernacular tongues of the people.'[20] Support for vernacular tongues includes both regional or ethnic as well as national languages, and Ngugi sees no need for any rivalry between them. In one of his more radical statements, he suggests that not only tribalism, but also ethnicity is outmoded: 'After all, traditional tribal or ethnic unities are irrelevant and reactionary now that the economic bases on which they rested have been removed.'[21] This undermining of ethnicity is not, however, a position which he retains.

'Return to the Roots' in *Writers in Politics* is Ngugi's first extended examination of the language question. He revisits Obi Wali's famous critique of the use of foreign languages, made originally in 1963, and notes the resistance of well-known individuals like Soyinka, Achebe and Mphahlele to his arguments (while acknowledging that people may change their position on such matters, as he himself has done).[22] Ngugi clearly wants to valorise, but not to romanticise, the use of indigenous languages (though whether he entirely avoids the pitfall of the latter is questionable); as he says: 'I do not wish of course to ascribe any mystical qualities to the mere fact of writing in African languages without regard to content and form.'[23] The choices writers make about which language to adopt need to involve an awareness of who their real audience is, as well as the use to which the language is put, and that has significant implications in the context of neo-colonial power relations at the level of culture.

It is *Decolonising the Mind*, however, which represents Ngugi's major intervention in the language debate. Its title has become a catchphrase in post-colonial studies, and its contents more argued over than read. The book is dedicated to 'all those who write in African languages', and preceded by a Statement in which Ngugi famously declares that it is 'my farewell to English as a vehicle for any of my writings. From now on it is Gikuyu and Kiswahili all the way.'[24] The arguments are not particularly new, being variations on the ones articulated in earlier essays; nor are they particularly complex; but they are developed at much greater length than before. Ngugi regards language as both a means of communication and as a carrier of people's culture, and thus to denigrate or damage a language has detrimental, potentially fatal effects on the culture which it carries. The converse also applies: to utilise the language creatively can rejuvenate the culture, and that is what post-colonial societies have required, and in many cases still do. Once again, however, it is the precise content of the language use – what is said or written – that is the crucial determinant of its political or cultural effectiveness:

> But writing in our languages per se – although a necessary first step in the correct direction – will not itself bring about the renaissance in African cultures if that literature does not carry the content of our people's anti-imperialist struggles to liberate their productive forces from foreign control.[25]

Ngugi's position is not one of linguistic essentialism, and so the converse of the fact that writing in African languages carries no guaranteed certificate of merit is that writing in European languages does not per se mean automatic linguistic or ideological contamination. What matters is the practical fact that if you write a novel in English, then that is one less properly African novel. In addition, choosing to write in English sends a message that European languages and cultural forms are the ones that count. Ngugi retains this position through to his most recent work, arguing that Europhone African literature:

> ... even at its most denunciatory, is also an unwitting accomplice to the repressive post-colonial state. Its ideological attitude towards the peasant and the worker and what they produce at the level of language and orature is not that different from the attitude of the state and the national merchant and bureaucratic bourgeoisie towards the same peasant and worker.[26]

This renders the politics of the (would-be) radical text somewhat more complex; it also places great weight on the reading of the ideological implications of formal or linguistic choice. By this severe standard, Ngugi himself, while championing peasants and workers and applauding their resistance in his later radical Anglophone novels (A Grain of Wheat, Petals of Blood) would presumably have been 'not that different' from the cynical, corrupt, neo-colonial bourgeoisie he was concerned to denounce. The severity of Ngugi's stance here also risks undermining his earlier position that the use of European languages does not necessarily equal ideological contamination.

In 'Language in African Literature: an aside to Ngugi', Joseph Mbele suggests that 'it has become almost unfashionable to challenge his [Ngugi's] views'.[27] It is not clear, however, what evidence he might find to support his contention, given the readiness of critics of all persuasions to attack Ngugi's views as parochial, self-defeating, nativist, or even, in the case of Achebe, virtually totalitarian. Certainly, neither Mbele nor Simon Gikandi, writing in the same issue of Research in African Literature, is deterred by this putative fashion. Gikandi's 'Ngugi's Conversion: Writing and the Politics of Language', an examination of perceived shifts in Ngugi's perspective on language from 'Return to the Roots' to Decolonising the Mind, is probably the most thought-provoking short study of Ngugi and the language question, but he appears so determined to find flaws in Ngugi's position that he frequently undoes his own argument. For instance, his response to Ngugi's assertion, 'literature as a process of thinking in images, utilises language and draws upon the collective experience – history – embodied in that language', is: 'this nativist/idealist notion of language ...'[28] though he provides no grounds for such a dismissal. Gikandi does unfortunately tend to attribute more to Ngugi than Ngugi actually says, or to draw conclusions which may not be warranted. Thus, for example, Ngugi talks about 'a return to the roots of our being in the languages and cultures and heroic histories of the Kenyan people'[29] and Gikandi turns it into 'the value of Being and the innate consciousness of collective culture'.[30] While the very idea of a 'return to the roots' might seem suspect to some, Gikandi's trick of capitalising Being gives it deeply phenomenological connotations which have nothing to do with Ngugi's Marxism or his notion of mere existence. Similarly, the non-materialist notion of 'innate consciousness' seems unrelated to anything Ngugi is saying. Gikandi aims to do something approaching an Althusserian symptomatic reading of Ngugi's argument, focusing on gaps, fissures and contradictions in his discourse and what they reveal, though he moves from identifying contradictions in the text to claiming contradictions in Ngugi's perceived motivation for his 'conversion' – whether mere pragmatism or intellectually justified. He also looks at Ngugi's indebtedness to Eurocentric concepts and sees him struggling to answer 'a question that continues to haunt cultural production in Africa: does the nation depend on a single unifying language to sustain its identity, or is the national space inherently polyglot?'[31] Some might suggest that African writers are in fact being haunted by a non-question: the nation space *is* inherently polyglot (and Ngugi enjoys listing the languages which inhabit Kenyan space); at the same time, nations, and more specifically nation-states, tend to prefer and prioritise the monoglot and the monologic for the purposes of the formation of (an illusion of) a unified national identity – and deploy political pressure to that end. In that context, Ngugi is happy to talk about 'the all-

Kenyan national language (i.e. Kiswahili) ...'[32] in the same sentence as he lists all the other languages. The many provocative points which Gikandi raises deserve a more extensive and detailed response than is possible here, but his article does stand out from other treatments of the language question, not least in the quality of its insights. Among the latter, Gikandi points to the contradictions in Ngugi's readiness to see Gikuyu as generating a unified, if not harmonious, view of the people, their lives, collective identity, etc. This – remarkably perhaps for Ngugi – omits any reference to the difference which class location or affiliation would make, and undoubtedly creates problems for his model of language and its functioning. It is a striking omission given his insistence on the need to retain an awareness of the class dimension.

A profound sense of the responsibility of writers, and intellectuals generally, which is central to the language debate, is of course not a new thing in Ngugi's writing. As we saw in the chapters on individual novels, it figures throughout his creative work; the same is true of the essays, which raise questions about writers in general, though the most urgent or painful instantiations are often in the post-colonial world. Even in an early piece like 'Towards a National Culture', Ngugi, as well as reviewing the (Fanonian) arguments about the need for writers to free themselves from Western intellectual hegemony, argues for practical and structural change:

> The universities and our schools should go to the countryside; there must be total involvement with the creative struggle of the peasants and workers. The present unhealthy, dangerous gap between intellectual and practical labour, between the rural and urban centres, would be bridged.[33]

In 'The Writer and His Past' in the same collection, Ngugi examines the complex relationship indicated in the title and demonstrates a willingness to cross entrenched disciplinary boundaries and debate 'literary' issues with historians. He even dares to disagree with them, criticising, for example, Gideon

Were's claim that the effect of colonialism on Africa was negligible. Ngugi worries that the strategically necessary concern with the past on the part of writers (necessary because colonialism did so much to deny the sense of a worthwhile African past, and even the physical evidence that one had existed), will distract them from more pressing problems:

> He [the African novelist] has already done something in restoring the African character to his history, to his past. But in a capitalist society the past has a romantic glamour; gazing at it ... is often a means of escaping the present. It is only in a socialist context that a look at yesterday can be meaningful in illuminating today and tomorrow.[34]

For Ngugi, social conditions mean that there are broadly two types of writers in any given historical period. The first group consists of those who believe in the status quo, in a static society, in timeless truths and universal values, and who play down the importance of history and the possibility of social transformation. The second group comprises those who have deliberately or instinctively acquired a more dialectical perspective on society which, as well as belief in the possibility and necessity of change, includes an awareness of the operations of power relations within societies (in class terms), and between them (particularly in this context in the shape of imperialism). This model is not as simplistic as it might appear, however, and Ngugi acknowledges that writers from the first group can produce perceptive social criticism, while those in the second group, including African novelists, can be severely hampered by their class-affiliated ideologies. Significantly, Ngugi recalls his own position of the early 1960s, looking forward to the time when African writers would have got over their obsession with colonialism, politics and the like, and moved on to producing novels in a more European mode. Ngugi may have developed a more useful outlook since then, but calls from writers and critics for post-colonial authors to give up their 'fixation' with colonialism and related issues have not gone away. In a sense, Ngugi's own experience of growing political awareness and changing perspectives goes against his model, which does tend to suggest fixed roles and politically or ideologically-allocated positions for writers. At the same time, we must recognise that Ngugi has always stressed the question of the choices faced by writers and intellectuals – above all, perhaps, in the post-colonial context – regarding whose side they are on. As he says in the Preface to *Writers in Politics*, however, there are circumstances in which writers do not have a choice, for instance in believing that they can transcend politics, or avoid taking sides: 'What he/ she cannot do is to remain neutral. Every writer is a writer in politics. The only question is what and whose politics?'[35]

In the title essay in *Writers in Politics*, Ngugi is perhaps more concerned with writers as products of their history than with what they have to say about it. Faced with the contradictory results of that history – a small black ruling class perpetuating neo-colonial conditions which oppress the majority of the population – many modern African writers 'retreat into individualism, mysticism and formalism', a retreat made all the more tempting no doubt because the alternative required of them is not easy.[36] Analytically, they should be aware of 'the global character of imperialism and the global dimension of the forces struggling against it …'; artistically, they must be 'very particular, very involved in a grain of sand, but must see the world, past, present and future, in that grain …'; politically, they must show commitment 'not to abstract notions of justice and peace, but the actual struggle of the African peoples to seize power'.[37]

In 'The Freedom of the Artist' in *Barrel of a Pen*, Ngugi looks at what happens to those writers, especially in post-colonial Kenya, who do take the side of the people. In the case of his friends, colleagues and collaborators, this has included official harassment, arrest, torture, imprisonment and exile. Considerable risks are also run by those whose 'popular' effort might seem altogether more modest, if not completely inoffensive. As an example, Ngugi cites a case which has strong echoes of his famous Kamiriithu theatre project: a play written by Kenyan schoolgirls under the direction of a nun (and therefore, one might assume, not especially revolutionary) enjoyed a degree of national success until it was translated into Gikuyu, whereupon performances were stopped, the headmistress was questioned by the police, girls were expelled, and the nun was deported, even though she was Kenyan.

While this type of state repression constitutes a clear curtailment of writers' freedom, there are also likely to be self-imposed limitations in operation, and following on from the 'stasis versus change' model of writers' perspectives mentioned above, Ngugi gives another binary image: 'The two world views have produced two types of artists: the poet laureate or the court singer to the status quo, and the trumpeter of a new world.'[38] While the 'court singers' may have greater freedom from repression by the ruling class (since their 'songs' are pleasing to them), their chosen role represents 'a state of self-imposed slavery'.[39] Ngugi also raises the question of whether any writer can meaningfully consider themselves free when their fellow intellectuals continue to be arrested and imprisoned. And the relationship is not just one between intellectuals; as Ngugi puts it in the revised edition of *Writers in Politics*, in a statement describing the maximal mutual responsibility:

> It is true that no writer or artist is free for as long as there is anybody in prison, exile, or a victim of death squads. But it is also true that none of us is free as long as there is any artist in prison or exile or a victim of death squads and state terrorism of any kind. The artist and society are bound to one another for ever.[40]

Much to Ngugi's anger and dismay, the persuasive power of this ethical imperative fails to move numbers of African or Kenyan intellectuals, who evince a depressing lack of solidarity:

> But in another sense, Kenyan artists are to blame for their present plight because of their complacency and indifference to their democratic rights as Kenyans. We have in the past adopted the attitude: every one for himself … We have never come together to voice those interests that bind us together as Kenyan patriotic artists.[41]

This vision of divisive self-interest on the part of those who should know better is striking in view of Ngugi's typical presentation of Kenyan communality; he does not, however, make clear whether he sees this condition as entirely the result of imported Western individualism, capitalist-derived social fragmentation, or other factors. A notable example of this lack of solidarity – especially when placed in the context of international protests and demonstrations on his behalf – are the attacks made on Ngugi during and after his detention by Kenyan writers and fellow academics, accusing him, among other things, of being an ideologue, a Gikuyu nationalist, and blindly pro-communist, of living in a fantasy world, and of going beyond the proper limits for a writer. Ngugi comments: 'To them [petty bourgeois intellectuals at the university] my detention proved them right in their caution and they could now hide their refusal to defend the democratic right of free expression by openly attacking me.'[42] Part of the fault lies in leaving the fight for freedom of expression almost entirely in the hands of writers and intellectuals, when as Ngugi points out in the quote above, it is a mutual responsibility, a struggle for all to undertake together.

A refusal to undertake the struggle almost guarantees the continuation of constraints and confinement for everyone. Though the precise mode of confinement may vary, the general lack of freedom, whether one is a writer or not, is a problem to which Ngugi returns throughout his recent collections of essays. Just as in the chapter on *Matigari* we saw him positing the exile of the writer as the paradigm case of a more generalised condition of exile and alienation experienced by contemporary Africans under neo-colonial regimes, so the constraining or imprisoning of intellectuals figures a more extensive confinement:

> Prison then is a metaphor for the post-colonial space, for even in a country where there are no military regimes, the vast majority can be described as being condemned to conditions of perpetual physical, social and psychic confinement.[43]

Despite the emphasis on a shared struggle, the image of one led by the artists often surfaces in Ngugi's essays, not least in his latest book *Penpoints, Gunpoints and Dreams*. In 'Art War with the State', rather than examining particular examples or strategies of state repression of artistic production, Ngugi seems to be concerned with positing an essential (and therefore ahistorical and unmaterialist) antagonism between states and the artists who inhabit them. The 'nature' of art and that of the state as Ngugi sees them are inherently at odds with one another. Part of the problem is that, on the 'art' side, Ngugi tends to slip between discussions of culture and art as if they were synonymous, while on the 'state' side he sometimes talks about the absolutist state, at others simply about the state. This can leave the reader confused about whether Ngugi sees all states as essentially absolutist, or whether the state-art antagonism only really exists in those states which are definitely absolutist, and secondly whether the antagonism is between the state and art, or the state and culture. Some explanation for this lack of clarity may be contained in Ngugi's statement that 'ultimately the complex tensions between the social and imaginative powers, between the art of the state and the state of art, can only be suggested through images and hence the overall title: *Penpoints, Gunpoints and Dreams*.'[44] The renunciation of an attempt to explain, in favour of suggestion via images, no doubt sides with the artistic, but does not necessarily do much for readerly comprehension. Similarly, Ngugi's desire to work with patterns – 'the art of the state and the state of art' and others which recur through the essay – may be more satisfactory in terms of rhetorical practice than cultural analysis. Similar chiastic patterns form the basis of the second piece in the book, on the politics of performance space: 'The war between art and the state is really a struggle between the power of performance in the arts and the performance of power by the state – in short, enactments of power.'[45] The focus on performance offers a different framework for examining the politics of radical theatre (including Kamiriithu) but Ngugi also includes a discussion of prison, official punishment and prison writings in relation to performances of power and resistance.

In contrast to the idea of a restorative history, one which engenders a renewed sense of collective identity and which we saw earlier, we find in the later collection *Moving the Centre* a more threatening, subversive history. What it particularly subverts is the desire of ruling classes, not least in post-colonial Africa, to halt social transformation (and in that respect, links up with the discussion of the attitude of writers to social change) 'but it is precisely because history is the result of struggle and tells of change that it is perceived as a threat by all the ruling strata in all the oppressive exploitative systems.'[46] One way for the ruling classes to cope with the threat is to control the production of history (which they have frequently done). In a manner which also applies to writing more generally, this situation produces particular versions of history and particular affiliations of historians, siding with, in Ngugi's terms, the oppressors or the oppressed. His conclusion on subversion is, it has to be said, somewhat problematic: 'History is subversive because *truth* is!'[47] This gives the impression that, rather than a discursive-political-institutional struggle, we are dealing with a simple choice between truth and lies. This is not a position which many historians, conservative or radical, would assent to as a description of how their discipline works; it also seems to posit a truth which is unitary, knowable and possessible. Nevertheless, like literary representations – which as Ngugi repeatedly points out, powerfully inform both our perceptions of the world and our actions in it – these competing versions of history, regardless of whether they contain 'truth' or not, certainly constitute the basis for cultural production, political mobilisation, and other forms of significant action. Similarly, whether or not the process is reducible to history as the ally of the oppressors versus history as the weapon of the oppressed, it is clear from the discussion in connection with *Petals of Blood* that there is a power struggle in progress here which is related to vested institutional and disciplinary interests, but which also has wider political implications.

A somewhat different aspect of the past – neither subversive nor simply restorative – is the educative past. Central to the pedagogic possibilities, in Ngugi's view, is the need to grasp both the positive and the negative elements in history, as he puts it in

'Learning from Our Ancestors: the Intellectual Legacy of Pan-Africanism': '... learning from our ancestors is not only when we uncritically glorify everything that has gone before us. It is not, in other words, simply the celebration of a past without a blemish.'[48] (This, if one disregards the rather unsettling implications of 'only' and 'simply', is a useful reminder that historical memory requires something other than communal hagiography as acceptable content.) For Ngugi, one of the most important lessons is of the cost to Africa of its disunity (and conversely, of the enormous potential of unity). Blame for some of the worst aspects of the history of the last four hundred years, covering the slave trade and colonialism, can, in Ngugi's eyes, be laid at the door of African disunity, though he tends to see the disunity as the direct result of different forms and stages of Western intervention, rather than as in any way already present in African societies: 'The ease with which African states will murder their own people can only be explained in terms of internalized racist values that express themselves in terms of self-hate.'[49] In contrast to the ongoing disunity, Ngugi examines the historical achievements, legacy and current potential of Pan-Africanism as unifying vision and movement. Although 'the literature produced by African writers over the last fifty years or so is the nearest thing we have to a Pan-African property',[50] much more might have been achieved by these writers and other intellectuals in terms of fostering unity if they had been expounding their ideas or writing their novels in indigenous languages.

At its broadest, Pan-Africanism is a global movement, embracing the whole of the African diaspora, but it is just one of the forms of progressive intra- and international solidarity whose possibilities Ngugi examines. Another notion which he is concerned to reanimate is that of an East African federation, which was very much part of the rhetoric, if not the practical policies, of the early post-independence period, but was wrecked by the incompatible directions taken by the participant nations – in particular, Tanzania under Nyerere towards socialism, and Kenya under Kenyatta into, in Ngugi's words, 'a classical neocolony, preferring its cosy relationship with the West as client state'.[51] Thirty years later, Museveni's Uganda and Moi's Kenya may be no closer ideologically, but the need for a federation in the face of the negative aspects of internationalism – capitalism, neo-colonialism – is greater than ever, while the basis for unity in geography, a common language (Kiswahili), and importantly for Ngugi, a common history of anti-colonial resistance, is still there.

Resistance is of course another of Ngugi's progressive internationalisms. As we have seen throughout this book, he is proud of Kenya's long tradition of resistance, and the majority of his works, fiction and non-fiction, make reference to it, and frequently contain lists of the heroes and heroines of that resistance. At the same time, he very much wants to emphasise the international, even universal, dimension – resistance as something like a shared human heritage, a common statement of refusal to forego basic human dignity in the face of violence or oppression: 'For this resistance [to imperialism] to be successful, it has to be waged at all the levels we have been talking about: economic, political, cultural and psychological ... For we are talking about nothing less than the right of all the peoples of the earth to be human.'[52] As imperialism has become a global phenomenon, so, of necessity for Ngugi, resistance to it takes place globally. Unfortunately, this does not happen in a co-ordinated manner – and certainly with nothing like the co-ordination which imperialism can muster when the need arises (even though it often advances in a haphazard way). Obviously, the more resistance could become integrated, the greater its chances of success, and the possibility creates a wonderful vision for Ngugi: 'The collapse of neo-colonialism and all the international and national structures of domination, dependencies, parasitisms (Nkrumah's last stage of imperialism), would see the birth of a new world, the beginnings of a truly universal human culture.'[53]

This – upbeat, oppositional, strongly optimistic, even utopian, as the endings of Ngugi's talks, essays and recent creative work have often been – may be an appropriate point at which to leave discussion of his non-fiction. The fact that critics continue to find such visionary moments aesthetically unconvincing or politically naive has clearly not deterred Ngugi so far. The epithet 'dreamer' is one which he has readily accepted, aligning himself with the Guyanese poet Martin Carter on the side of all those who 'do not sleep to dream, but dream to change the world'[54] and remaining secure in the conviction that, in the words of another famous late twentieth-century dreamer, he is 'not the only one'.

Critical overview and conclusion

MORE than thirty-five years of critical writing on Ngugi has created a huge body of work. Carole Sicherman's invaluable bibliography, covering the first twenty-five years, contains almost two thousand entries.[1] The rate of critical output has also increased dramatically as Ngugi's status has grown – the years 1980–87 account for over half of the critical entries in Sicherman's bibliography – so that an up-to-date version would be enormous, and a true critical overview would almost need to be an entire book in its own right. In this situation a single chapter can do little more than indicate the breadth of critical debate – and we can take it as read that any work of Ngugi's will produce a wide range of frequently irreconcilable critical opinions. The chapters on Ngugi's novels and plays in this book have tried to indicate some of the representative critical attitudes, as well as the fact that his work is both the site of, and the occasion for, ideological power struggles at the level of cultural production and interpretation. Disagreements over his writing began as early as 1963, with the argument in the journal *Transition* between critics Gerald Moore and Peter Nazareth over Ngugi's play *The Black Hermit,* and have continued unabated.

In view of the extreme difficulty of providing anything like a full critical overview in this chapter, we will follow the pattern of the previous chapter and work with a restricted but representative sample of material. In this case, the focus will be just one paradigmatic novel, but one which has been criticised from positions which cover almost the entire range of available possibilities: metropolitan and Third World; Africanist and 'universalist'; academic and non-academic; 'high' cultural and populist; theoretical and anti-theory; 'literature as art' versus 'writing as politicised cultural praxis'. Rather than simply offering a list of what critics have said, the aim here is both to illustrate the range of important critical positions, and to attempt to engage with them. (This may sometimes risk giving the unfortunate appearance of a relentless effort to defend Ngugi at all costs, but the intention, on the contrary, is to offer a sense of the debates.)

Petals of Blood occupies a pivotal position in Ngugi's fictional writing: his last novel in English, his longest and most complex 'traditional' novel, it marks the intensification both of the politicisation of his writing and of the divergence of responses to it. As such, it focuses substantial issues of critical reading and reception in a way which none of his other works can equal. Some of the critical polarisation results from the fact that, as a novel centrally concerned with modes of resistance, one of its own acts of textual resistance is to its easy consumption by traditional critics or standardised approaches which had deemed Ngugi's earlier novels eminently acceptable. John Updike's assessment is typical of an inflexible high-culturalist attitude unsettled by an apparently deviant text. Updike, for example, considers the novel aesthetically deficient -'tedious and implausible'[2] – and finds Ngugi's use of Gikuyu words and phrases in the early pages of the novel almost an act of aggression against the Western reader.

David Maughan Brown discusses at some length the powerful effects of Western aesthetic ideologies – transmitted through the university system in Africa and reinforced in the work of literary critics – on writers, even those like Ngugi who were gradually attempting to develop more radical positions and practices. Commenting on a critic whose verdict is that 'Ngugi's sensitivity to the human motives on both sides of the conflict is (to the European reader at least) one of his greatest strengths as a novelist ...', Maughan Brown says:

Hower's projection of a monolithic 'European' critical response is symptomatic. 'Balance', 'restraint', 'patience', 'universality', the absence of polemic, and 'sensitivity to the human motives on both sides' are what the critics look for, and, not coincidentally, what they tend to find in *Weep Not, Child*, and *A Grain of Wheat*, but not *Petals of Blood*.[3]

As we saw in the last chapter, Ngugi's negative assessment of universality was the result of the Western habit of presenting their own very partial perspective as the one with universal relevance, not least in the realm of the aesthetic.

One of the more prevalent assumptions of this type of criticism is of the incompatibility of the aesthetic and the political in a work of literature, and of the inevitably deleterious effect of the latter on the former. For many critics, *Petals of Blood* is where Ngugi allows politics to ruin everything. C. B. Robson is typical of those who feel that Ngugi has failed aesthetically in *Petals of Blood*, and his praise for the first three novels – e.g., 'he presents fundamental human concerns in a form which gives his work immediacy, artistic unity and a universal dimension'[4] – does not extend to *Petals of Blood*, where Ngugi is seen to transgress all the critical desiderata listed by Maughan Brown: restraint, universality, balance, and absence of polemic:

One of the novel's weaknesses is the way in which it conveys a great deal of information. Conveying inform-ation is a legitimate part of a novelist's role, but in *Petals of Blood* Ngugi goes beyond what is acceptable in fiction: he is giving us polemic. Basically it is a question of balance …[5]

Where the limits of the 'acceptable' lie, what determines where the dividing line between literature and polemic falls, is not clear, though the implication is that 'we all know'.

Robson also criticises what he sees as a lack of psychological depth in the characters, and their reduction to 'allegorical figures'. This is a variant on a complaint, often found in early criticism of African writing of the 60s and 70s, that authors seemed unwilling or unable to create 'the psychological and emotional depth which the novel demands',[6] where the notion that African writers might have a valid alternative perspective on psychology, or other agendas in which complex character psychology was of no consequence, rarely seemed to occur. In addition, Robson, perhaps because he is unhappy with the radicalised writing produced by Ngugi in the late 70s, repeats the suggestion that 'Ngugi and writers such as lo Liyong and p'Bitek represent a literary establishment that has performed a valuable duty and is now about to be replaced by younger, more appropriate talents.'[7] (The idea that Ngugi represented an outdated literary establishment might be seen as unconsciously revelatory here.)

Although he might be considered part of the literary-critical establishment, Andrew Gurr's assessment of *Petals of Blood* is generally more positive, seeing it, unlike other 'political' fourth novels by Achebe and Naipaul to which he compares it, as a consistent development of Ngugi's earlier work, where the political does not constitute automatic decline.[8] Similarly, G. D. Killam feels that '*Petals of Blood* affirms the consistency of Ngugi's themes and attitudes.'[9] Along with numbers of other critics, he comments on the implications of the echoes of Yeats' poem *The Second Coming* in the novel's section headings, but where the majority want (problematically) to read this in terms of Yeats' concept of cyclical time (to which we shall return later), Killam focuses on 'the disillusion of civilisation, the home not of Christ in a Second Coming but of anti-Christ'.[10]

In addition to Gurr, Cook and Okenimkpe feel that *Petals of Blood* marks progress from the earlier works, in this case in terms of structure and 'symmetry of form',[11] but at the same time, unlike the generally non-judgmental Killam, they offer forthright opinions and evaluations of author, characters or events. At times, these are more than forthright; for instance, while neither Munira nor his wife may be particularly well-adjusted individuals, neither seems to deserve the epithet 'psychopathic' (not even Munira in arsonist mode) which Cook and Okenimkpe bestow. Also, a number of these opinions appear to be unsubstantiated: for example, it is difficult to see how the claim 'the police investigation, upon which the whole plot hangs, nominally underwrites the process of law and order, but implicitly sympathises with the assassination which expresses public indignation at the repression of legitimate aspirations', might be supported, even if the novel might want us as readers to be indignant at injustice and (possibly) sympathise with the retribution.[12] Firstly, Inspector Godfrey who leads, and indeed embodies, that investigation, is an ardent supporter of, and believer in, the system which the murdered men represent and which it is also his job to protect. Secondly, the central characters who are implicated in murder (Abdulla, Munira, Wanja) act principally as a result of motivations which are private rather than public, while the novel's representative of 'public' opposition, Karega (despite being, in Inspector Godfrey's eyes 'worse than murderers'), has nothing to do with the killing, and explicitly rejects 'the elimination of individuals'.[13]

The section devoted to *Petals of Blood* in Simon Gikandi's *Reading the African Novel* offers a discussion which bridges literary-critical and political concerns in a generally exemplary way for such a short piece. Gikandi provides a detailed analysis of the main characters in the novel, but links this to political projects or possibilities. Like the other critics mentioned, Gikandi discerns – and evaluates as artistic failing on Ngugi's part – inconsistencies between the 'nature' of certain characters and the ideas or ideologies which they present (though he may not agree with others about precisely which characters are inconsistent). As an example of inconsistency, he mentions Munira suddenly pondering the effects of colonialism and modernisation – though in fact even Munira recognises these as 'alien' thoughts. The major failing of the novel, in Gikandi's eyes, results from excessive authorial intrusiveness, which can lead to 'incredible' characters, or to unacceptably blatant statements, such as Karega's 'moral conclusion "whenever any of us is degraded and humiliated, even the smallest child, we are all humiliated and degraded because it has to do with human beings" which is a naked ideological cliché'[14] – though some might choose to read this as a laudable affirmation of common humanity along the lines of John Donne's famous sermon.

One of the strongest attacks on *Petals of Blood*, and one of the most direct challenges to critical approaches to African novels, comes in Stuart Crehan's 'The Politics of the Signifier: Ngugi wa Thiong'o's *Petals of Blood*'. Crehan's discussion of the novel is more theoretically informed than others mentioned so far, drawing on Barthes and Bakhtin, semiotics and narratology, though the grounds for his criticism of the novel may not be all that different. Rather surprisingly perhaps, he feels that 'Critics on the whole have been fairly kind to *Petals of Blood*'[15] – though that may only be relative to the severity with which, in his eyes, they might have written about it. More seriously, though,

> Most critics of the novel seem noticeably bashful about honestly confronting it as a work of imaginative literature … there is something insidiously dishonest – even puritanically self-denying – about a critical practice that represses the reader's own aesthetic response for the sake of some 'higher truth' – a practice that some African writers have positively encouraged.[16]

There is the (worrying) assumption in Crehan's article that any honest response would necessarily register the same kind of dissatisfaction as he does, but his call for critical honesty is hard to object to. (Whether privileging the aesthetic response over the 'higher truth' – whatever that might be – is axiomatically the only proper or honest procedure is another question.) Crehan also argues that the entire text – its structure and strategies, as well as its content or message – needs to be analysed; and again, as a basic position, that seems unobjectionable. A potential problem arises, however, over whether the grounds for Crehan's critique are demonstrable, or exist only at the level of assertion. (This carries its own unsettling echoes of the elitist cultural politics disguised as consensus in F. R. Leavis' famous 'This is so, is it not?' – it being impossible to dissent and still count as a sensitive/honest/right-thinking critic of literature.) It remains to be resolved whether Ngugi's writing in *Petals of Blood* is indisputably monotonous, infelicitous, melodramatising or dogmatic, as claimed by Crehan, or whether that has more to do with the latter's rhetorical and persuasive power.

Contrary to the argument regarding the multiplicity of voices and viewpoints advanced in the chapter on *Petals of Blood* in this book, Crehan regards the novel, in Bakhtinian terms, as monologic:

> Monologic discourse does not spring from the people, since it is always the voice of an Author-God we hear, whether as omniscient extradiegetic narrator, or 'disguised' as the represented speech and inner speech of intradiegetic narrators and characters.[17]

Despite the fact that earlier in the article he had distanced himself from the idea of an Author-God and repudiated the notion of complete authorial control, Crehan is here attacking what he sees as Ngugi relentlessly forcing his personal point of view on all of his characters. The problem, however, is that, in spite of the presence of intertexts, other discourses and ideologies – the social heteroglossia with which Bakhtin is concerned – and in spite of the fact that, as Bakhtin says 'the word in language is half someone else's',[18] there remains the sense in which any novel has to be the voice of its Author-God, though presumably some manage to perfect their disguise and convince critics like Crehan that this is not the case.

The reductivism which Crehan sees at work in relation to narrative voice turns up in other areas too:

> Translating moral complexities into certainties entails a melodramatised, simplified scheme. Between the damned (vile seducers like Kimeria) and the redeemed (heroes who have gained Eternal Life in the hearts of the masses, or strong, simple, noble hearted peasants such as Nyakinyua) are those whose hearts are a battleground of opposing moral forces (Munira, Karega, Abdulla, Wanja). Such a scheme involves a set of easy reflexes: moral denunciation of wicked and depraved exploiters on the one hand, and a sentimental idealization of the exploited masses on the

other. From a political standpoint, this can be a very dangerous attitude, since it over-simplifies and distorts the nature of the struggle by turning it into a mere contest between good and evil. Far from raising consciousness, this can actually disarm the masses. Sentimentality and melodrama thus work against any attempt at an objective analysis of class formation and historical change – an analysis which the story line of *Petals of Blood* tries to illustrate – by confusing economic relations with moral ones.[19]

Among the many questions to ask of this forceful analysis is whether – even if we grant, as some critics would be unwilling to do, that extensive (over)simplification is what is happening in the novel – situations and issues are necessarily always so complex. For example, if individuals like Kimeria and Chui are – objectively, demonstrably – cheating, exploiting and oppressing substantial numbers of their fellow Kenyans, wherein lies the moral complexity? Does their economic activity *not* carry a moral dimension? (After all, Marxist opposition to capitalist extraction of surplus value from the labour of the proletariat has to be morally/ethically based, since at a simple economic level the practice 'works' extremely well.) There is also a potential problem with the class-located interest in perceiving things as complex: 'the middle-class habit of complicated retrospection, typified in Munira …'[20] as Crehan puts it, is not automatically self-recommending, still less self-legitimating (not least because it is part of a mind-set which habitually denies complexity to those who do not belong in class or racial terms). It further needs to be asked whether simplification necessarily equals melo-dramatising and sentimentalising, and whether, far from dis-arming the masses, a certain simplification may not have the opposite effect – it being far easier to mobilise politically around clearly-defined positions than intractable moral dilemmas.

One area where Ngugi would certainly endorse Crehan's call for greater honesty is in discussions of the past. As we saw in the chapter on *Petals of Blood*, the importance of the past – whether immediate, recent or distant; whether publicly acknowledged or, especially, individually or collectively repressed – is central to understanding the novel. We saw, for example, Karega's dissatisfaction with attitudes to the past which were retrogressive, simply nostalgic or over-romanticising. To argue, then, as Cook and Okenimkpe do, that this constitutes 'a radical rejection of the African past',[21] would on the one hand seem to make nonsense of Ngugi's constant evocation and positive highlighting of the past, and on the other to ignore the evidence of the passage they have just quoted where Karega says that the past is important as something to be learned from, to assist present and future actions. Similarly, Karega's rejection encompasses Western-affiliated or Western-inspired narratives of history, but certainly not every version of history or experience embodied in African accounts of oppression and resistance.

The past and Ngugi's methods for dealing with it clearly cause Cook and Okenimkpe some difficulty; for instance they feel that: 'he lectures us somewhat sententiously on history', or treats it much too abstractly, or in 'words and phrases which are bare of imaginative force ... particularly so in earnest passages of retrospective narrative or historical background'.[22] One could argue against the charge of abstraction that in fact Ngugi embodies a great deal of Kenyan historical experience across the generations in his characters, but the real problem arises because he allows characters to reflect on and analyse historical situations and processes, and this above all makes the novel too obvious, or dogmatic, or insufficiently literary, for many critics.

Just as elements of the dominant aesthetic ideologies still persist in writers who are radicalising their practice, so we can find them (strongly present) in those radical critics, or critics writing in radical journals, who would not identify themselves with the literary-critical old guard. Since to an extent the latter's criticisms might be anticipated, it is worth looking in a little detail at the problems of radical critics. In 'The Divergence of Art and Ideology in the Later Novels of Ngugi wa Thiong'o: A Critique' in *Ufahamu: Journal of the African Activist Association*, Lisa Curtis focuses the negative dimension of that critique on *Petals of Blood*. Her criticism rests on certain assumptions, both generalising and specific to the novel, against the normative standards of which Ngugi can be judged to have failed:

> Liberal humanism lends itself to 'conventional' novel forms in a way that dogmatic political writing does not ... This raises the question whether the 'novel' with its conventional tendency to understatement is the appropriate form to embody explicit political dogma. *A Grain of Wheat* stands apart from Ngugi's later novels in the way in which it universalises the human struggle for order and meaning in a changing world.[23]

Both at the general and the specific levels, her assumptions reproduce the traditional aesthetic ideology questioned by Maughan Brown, and as such, perhaps need no further comment. Like Stuart Crehan, Curtis discusses the question of narrative voice in the novel, and finds different problems with it: 'The fact that Ngugi is unable to sustain the collective narrative voice is perhaps itself indicative of the sense in which the traditional African society he describes is resistant to the imposition of Marxist social categories.'[24] This represents a fascinating leap from implied failure of individual authorial technique to asserted failure of the social applicability or analytical purchase of general theory in a relationship both causal and mimetic. No evidence is offered, however, as to the ways in which, or the reasons why, traditional African society would resist analysis in Marxist terms. In addition, it is not clear that Ngugi is 'unable to sustain' a collective voice, though she has earlier offered a suggestion as to why that should be the case: 'The intrusion of personal motives on ostensibly social preoccupations ... significantly undermine the intention of collectivist expression.'[25] Other than the undeniable fact that most of the narration comes through Munira's reminiscences and the omniscient narrative voice, and that the communal voice is therefore marginal, there is no sign of a tried-and-failed technique on Ngugi's part.

One of Curtis's fundamental accusations against *Petals of Blood* relates to her understanding of history. Unlike in *A Grain of Wheat*, it is alleged, 'past events are seen as part of an inexorable cycle of historical determinism.' In addition, 'the historical overview which informs *Petals of Blood* is equally inflexible. This view is that all men in the world are either exploiters or exploited ...'[26] There are numerous other assertions along these lines, but perhaps these will suffice for the sake of demonstration. Taking the second quote first, this rigid binary can in no way be said to constitute a 'historical overview': while Kenyans were obviously exploited under colonialism and continue to be so under neo-colonialism, the text reveals the philosophy of 'eat or be eaten' as precisely symptomatic of the degraded state of (part of) contemporary society, embodied in the new parasitic ruling class or in Wanja at her most despairing, and thus neither eternal nor inflexible. Previously society did not function in this way; it now needs to (re)discover a more modern or post-colonial version of those same collaborative relations.

Still on the subject of historical determinism, Curtis quotes at length a passage from the novel:

> From Agu and Agu, Tene wa Tene, from long before the Manjiru generation, the highway had seen more than its fair share of adventurers from the north and north-west. Solomon's suitors for myrrh and frankincense; Zeus's children in a royal hunt for the seat of the sun-god of the Nile; scouts and emissaries of Genghis Khan; Arab geographers and also hunters for slaves and ivory; soul and gold merchants from Gaul and from Bismarck's Germany; land pirates and human game hunters from Victorian and Edwardian England: they had all passed here bound for a kingdom of plenty, driven sometimes by holy zeal, sometimes by a genuine thirst for knowledge and the quest for the spot where the first man's umbilical cord was buried, but more often by mercenary commercial greed and love of the wanton destruction of those with a slightly different complexion from theirs. They had come wearing different masks and guises, and God's children had, through struggle, survived every onslaught, every land- and soul-grabbing empire, and continued their eternal wrestling with nature and with their separate gods and mutual selves.[27]

This is taken to express 'patterns of historical inexorability', 'the relentless unfolding of historical purpose', and 'the terms of historical determinism'.[28] The principal mistake here, however, is to confuse historical repetition and historical inevitability; this parallels those critics over-eager to read Ngugi's use of Yeats' *The Second Coming* as an endorsement of Yeats' theory of history as cyclical – a vision whose inescapable nature would be anathema to a historical materialist like Ngugi, and Curtis herself, though she does not mention Yeats in this context, also regards Ngugi as using cyclical patterns. If, however, society were subject to ineluctable cycles of eternal return, that would make it precisely the sort of society which, as discussed in the last chapter, is in Ngugi's opinion the dream of ruling classes everywhere, where change is undesirable, unnecessary, or, best of all, impossible:

> Throughout history there have been two conflicting world views. The first sees the world of nature and man as static and fixed. Or if it moves at all, it is in cycles, repetitions of the same motions. Any concession to evidence or demonstration of previous movement in history is twisted to prove that the logic in all the previous movements was to arrive at the present fixed status quo. This is the world view of all the ruling classes ...[29]

There *is* a debt in the long passage from *Petals of Blood*, though it is not to Yeats' cosmic cycles; Ngugi is clearly drawing on two famous statements from the early pages of *Heart of Darkness*, though Conrad is hardly a writer associated with historical determinism. Another point to note is that the repetition in the passage is repetition within a framework of considerable variation, and that, even for Ngugi in his 'rigid' or 'dogmatic' Marxist mode, a wide range of motivation is ascribed to the outsiders – even including a 'genuine search for knowledge' – which does not fit a model of determinism. Perhaps most important is the final sentence, which Curtis does not quote, and which stresses the repeated fact of agency and adaptation on the part of Africans. The image of people making their own history, not in circumstances chosen by them but in part given by external forces, is on the one hand another famous echo (less obviously than the Conrad), of Marx, and, on the other, anything but an image of determinism at work. The crucial thing is to find ways of living and interacting which obviate or minimise the possibility of unwelcome repetitions, though for Curtis this is doomed from the start: 'The relentless cycles of time assert themselves at all levels of plot and narrative, undermining the revolutionary theme which finds expression in images of rebirth.'[30] If, however, we are dealing neither with cyclical time nor relentless patterns, then the past becomes more than a matter of mere fate to be undergone yet again, and positive change is possible. That possibility is enhanced when the final 'revolutionary' image is not one of (organic or mystical) rebirth, but human co-operation, solidarity and resistance – despite Curtis's conviction that 'the unity of workers, which we have seen only through the eyes of Karega, is as remote a possibility as a surfeit of Christian love and charity among the industrial magnates.'[31] As with the earlier 'failure' of Ngugi's Marxism, it is not clear whether Curtis is talking strictly about the world of the novel (where this impossible unity is already manifesting itself), or the 'real' world, where indeed its existence is altogether more of a problem.

One of the interesting things about Curtis's article is its combination of normative judgements about both literature and politics (Ngugi's later novels falling short on both counts). Some radical critics, such as Grant Kamenju, are not interested in the aesthetic dimension at all. In 'Petals of Blood as a Mirror of the African Revolution', Kamenju adopts an explicitly Leninist frame of reference, and analyses elements in the novel in a basically mimetic-representational manner.[32] Among the places where this breaks down is in relation to the title: it is not clear how Petals of Blood can be a mirror of the revolution (rather than a prediction), the revolution not having occurred yet. An example of Kamenju's lack of interest in purely aesthetic evaluation is indicated by the fact that both he and Peter Nazareth in the same collection quote the same passage from the later stages of the novel concerning Abdulla's hallucinatory thoughts before he makes the decision to kill Kimeria.[33] For

Nazareth, this is an example of Ngugi giving completely inappropriate thoughts and information to 'non-intellectual' characters (which therefore constitutes an aesthetic failing on the part of the author); for Kamenju, however, it is simply a useful picture of the relation of neo-colonial ruling classes to their foreign masters.

The question of history is important not only to Ngugi; indeed, for Alamin Mazrui and Lupenga Mphande it is an imperative for writers, especially African and activist ones like Ngugi. Mazrui and Mphande call for a radicalised use of history as a revolutionary weapon, and examine the ways in which Ngugi's challenges to conservative historiographic and novelistic practices might fit such a model. They consider 'the novel as a mode of historical discourse', but unfortunately their conception of the novel as (unacceptably) constituted by 'objective descriptions of reality' and stream of consciousness is inadequate, since stream of consciousness is hardly a defining feature of novelistic practice, even in the twentieth century, while accurate description of reality (however problematic a concept it may be) has been considered an acceptable goal by very many African activist writers. They also say 'For history to serve as a weapon in creative literature, a writer must transcend the boundaries of mere description of reality and negate the notion of individual consciousness.'[34] In *Petals of Blood*, however (which Mazrui and Mphande praise), Ngugi is concerned to show the formative effects of social movements or historical forces on his characters, and although they may even to an extent function as representative Lukacsian 'types', Wanja, Abdulla and the others remain very much individuals. Even Karega, who does the best job of subordinating his individual needs to the common struggle, still possesses a distinctly individual consciousness.

The most extensive and useful discussion of the question of history is Carole Sicherman's 'Ngugi wa Thiong'o and the Writing of Kenyan History', and like Mazrui and Mphande she concentrates on Ngugi's treatment of Mau Mau. Also like Mazrui and Mphande she claims a different historical practice for Ngugi, but in contrast to them she shows in some detail what this consists of, and is prepared both to praise and to criticise aspects of it. She notes both a growing attention to Kenyan history from *A Grain of Wheat* onwards, and in *Petals of Blood* a lack of distinction between fiction and non-fiction (with unfortunate aesthetic consequences). Importantly, *Petals of Blood* marks an interest in 'non-standard' models of what count as historical sources: 'The weight Ngugi gives to what "is said", to "rumour" and "gossip" as agents in forming the imaginative life of his people, makes it clear that he knows that actual historical force of what "is said" – its role in politics. Myths made things happen during the Emergency.'[35] This can be seen as an index of the growing importance of the popular, the oral and the marginalised in Ngugi's work.

Only slightly less unacceptable to traditional historians than rumour and gossip as source material are legends. Just before the long Conradian-style passage quoted above, Ngugi discusses the state of historical knowledge and historiography in Kenya, and finds them unsatisfactory: 'For there are many questions about our history which remain unanswered. Our present day historians, following on similar themes yarned out by defenders of imperialism, insist we only arrived here yesterday.'[36] In the absence of appropriate or useful work by Kenyan historians – and, remarkably for a work of fiction, Ngugi names those he is unhappy with, the most respected in the Kenyan establishment: Professors Bethwell Ogot, Godfrey Muriuki, Gideon Were and William Ochieng – he concludes that there is no alternative but to rely on 'legends passed from generation to generation', supplemented by up-to-date archaeological and linguistic evidence and reading between the lines of colonial accounts. The fact that Ngugi puts legends at the top of the list is a clear rebuff to what he regards as the 'neo-colonial' history establishment. The establishment in turn has responded with denunciations of him, particularly from professors Ochieng and Ogot.

The crux of the dispute is of course the continuing problem of how to write the history of Mau Mau – or whether to write at all, given President Moi's statement in 1986 that there should be no historical account of Mau Mau whatsoever. Mau Mau, whether understood as the culmination of centuries of indigenous resistance, or frustrated Gikuyu aspirations, or the first of the great African anti-colonial struggles, or a fratricidal war, or a national movement of independence, or the clearest manifestation of the inherent barbarism of Africans, or a movement which demanded reparation for losses suffered by the ordinary people, or, more recently, as that which must be disavowed by the Kenyan ruling class, is an issue which has divided Africans from Europeans, Kenyans from Kenyans, historians from novelists, and historians among themselves. Neo-colonial Kenyans are not the only historians who are uneasy about Ngugi's approach: John Lonsdale and Bruce Berman treat him somewhat contradictorily – at times they seem content to quote him with approval, but in the end they confine him to the camp of the 'radicals' (for them the producers of the worst kind of history): 'Ideological heroism has been demanded most determinedly of the evidence by those who have least studied it, who can indeed sneer at those who bury Mau Mau "in a heap of footnotes".'[37] (The unnamed target here is Ngugi – author of the footnotes comment – and the tone remarkable, coming from someone wishing to occupy the scholarly high ground in the debate.) The urgent problem for Ngugi and others, however, is not simply the burying of Mau Mau under footnotes but the continuing official attempt to bury it altogether, erasing it from both scholarly and popular memory.

Ngugi's effort here and in all his subsequently published work can be seen as part of what Walter Benjamin called 'the fight for the oppressed past'. For Benjamin, 'the tradition of the oppressed teaches us that the "state of emergency" in which we live is not the exception but the rule. We must attain to a conception of history that is in keeping with this insight.'[38] In the Kenyan context, the exceptional state of the Emergency, the Mau Mau war, becomes the daily state of emergency of the repressive neo-colonial regime. Ngugi's conception of history may not be the most fashionable in its Marxist persistence, but it is certainly in keeping with this aspect of the realities of his country. An acute awareness of the danger represented by the production of a version of history which serves the interests of the ruling class is something which Ngugi shares with Benjamin:

> Historical materialism wishes to retain that image of the past which unexpectedly appears to man singled out by history at a moment of danger. The danger affects both the content of the tradition and its receivers. The same threat hangs over both: that of becoming a tool of the ruling classes. In every era the attempt must be made to wrest tradition away from a conformism that is about to overpower it. Only that historian will have the gift of fanning the spark of hope in the past who is firmly convinced that *even the dead* will not be safe from the enemy if he wins. And this enemy has not ceased to be victorious.[39]

After all that we have seen of Ngugi, it is unnecessary to labour the point that although the enemy – trans-national capitalism and its local intermediaries – has not ceased to be victorious, the effort – through writing, through cultural activities of all kinds – to counter that success, to keep the spark of hope alive, continues unchecked.

Notes

Chapter 1

1 Jomo Kenyatta, *Facing Mount Kenya* (Oxford, Heinemann, 1979, first published 1938), p. 26.

2 Ngugi, interview, in Carole Sicherman, *Ngugi wa Thiong'o: The Making of a Rebel* (London, Hans Zell, 1990), p. 20.

3 Ngugi, *Moving the Centre* (London, James Currey, 1993), p. 139.

4 Ngugi, interview, in Sicherman, *Ngugi wa Thiong'o*, p. 23.

5 *Ibid.*, p. 23.

6 Ngugi, *Moving the Centre*, p. 142.

7 Ngugi, 'Church, Culture and Politics', in *Homecoming* (London, Heinemann, 1972), p. 31.

8 *Ibid.*, p. 35.

9 David Diop, 'Contribution to the Debate on National Poetry', *Présence Africaine*, 6 (1956), p. 23.

10 Ngugi, *Detained: A Writer's Prison Diary* (Oxford, Heinemann, 1981), p. 8.

11 Ngugi, *Barrel of a Pen* (Trenton N.J., Africa World Books, 1983), p. 46.

12 Ngugi, 'From the Corridors of Silence', in *Moving the Centre*, p. 102.

13 Tami Alpert, 'Ngugi by telephone' in Charles Cantalupo (ed.), *The World of Ngugi wa Thiong'o* (Trenton N.J., Africa World Press, 1995), p. 231.

14 Michel Foucault, *History of Sexuality*, Vol. 1 (Harmondsworth, Penguin, 1981), p. 95.

Chapter 2

1   Homi K. Bhabha (ed.), *Nation and Narration* (London, Routledge, 1990).

2   Edward Said, *Culture and Imperialism* (London, Chatto & Windus, 1993), pp. 40, 82.

3   Chinua Achebe, *Hopes and Impediments; Selected Essays 1965–87* (Oxford, Heinemann, 1988), p. 30.

4   G. W. F. Hegel, *The Philosophy of History* (New York, Dover, 1956), p. 99.

5   Ngugi, *Moving the Centre* (London, James Currey, 1995), pp. 109–10.

6   Fredric Jameson, 'Third World Literature in the Era of Multinational Capitalism', *Social Text*, Fall (1986), pp. 65–88.

7   Aijaz Ahmad, *In Theory: Classes, Nations, Literatures* (London, Verso, 1992), pp. 95–122.

8   Basil Davidson, *The Black Man's Burden: Africa and the Curse of the Nation-State* (London, James Currey, 1992), p. 115.

9   Aimé Césaire, *Discourse on Colonialism* (New York, Monthly Review Press, 1972), p. 57. Césaire has in mind here the kind of criticisms which people like Fanon and himself were making of a (Eurocentric) humanism which pretends to universality but which operates a racially-exclusive model of the 'human'.

10 Frantz Fanon, *The Wretched of the Earth* (Harmondsworth, Penguin, 1967), p. 142.

11 *The River Between*, though published the year after *Weep Not, Child*, was in fact written before it.

12 Sir Charles Eliot, quoted in Carole Sicherman, *Ngugi wa Thiong'o: The Making of a Rebel* (London, Hans Zell, 1990), pp. 271–2.

13 Hardinge, quoted in Bruce Berman and John Lonsdale, *Unhappy Valley* (London, James Currey, 1992), p. 19.

14 Berman and Lonsdale, *Unhappy Valley*, p. 13.

15 *Ibid.*, p. 21.

16 Benedict Anderson, *Imagined Communities* (London, Verso, 1983), p. 15.

17 Eric Hobsbawm and Terence Ranger, *The Invention of Tradition* (Cambridge University Press, 1983).

18 Jomo Kenyatta, *Facing Mount Kenya* (Oxford, Heinemann, 1979), p. 134.

19   Elleke Boehmer, 'The Master's Dance to the Master's Voice', *Journal of Commonwealth Literature*, 26:1 (1991), pp. 192–3.

20   *Ibid.*, p. 193.

21   Ngugi, *Detained: A Writer's Prison Diary* (Oxford, Heinemann, 1981), p. 106.

22   Abdul JanMohamed, *Manichean Aesthetics* (Amherst, University of Massachusetts Press, 1983), p. 5.

23   Ato Sekyi-Otu, 'The Refusal of Agency: The Founding Narrative and Waiyaki's Tragedy in *The River Between*', *Research in African Literatures*, 16 (1985), p. 167.

24   *Ibid.*, p. 167.

25   At the social level, monologism represents the attempt – particularly by ruling classes, but also by other powerful forces – to limit the naturally dialogic nature of interaction, to restrict what can be said or meant to their preferred options, and to silence other (especially oppositional) voices. See Mikhail Bakhtin, *The Dialogic Imagination* (Austin, University of Texas Press, 1981).

26   Berman and Lonsdale, *Unhappy Valley*, p. 319.

27   *Ibid.*, p. 319.

28   *Ibid.*, p. 322.

29   Werner Glinga, '*The River Between* and Its Forerunners', *World Literature Written in English*, 26:2 (1986), p. 226.

30   See David Maughan Brown, *Land, Freedom and Fiction: History and Ideology in Kenya* (London, Zed, 1985), chapter 8.

31   Louis Althusser, 'Ideology and Ideological State Apparatuses', in *Essays on Ideology* (London, Verso, 1984).

32   Kenyatta, *Facing Mount Kenya*, p. 21.

33   Maughan Brown, *Land, Freedom and Fiction*, p. 225.

34   *Ibid.*, p. 233.

35   Ngugi, *The Black Hermit* (Oxford, Heinemann, 1968), pp. 64–5.

36   *Ibid.*, p. 73.

37   Charles Nnolim, 'Structure and Theme in Ngugi wa Thiong'o's *A Grain of Wheat*', in G. D. Killam (ed.), *Critical Perspectives on Ngugi wa Thiong'o* (Washington, Three Continents Press, 1984), p. 218. While it would be possible to refute such an assessment point by point, that type of exercise lies outside the scope of this book.

38   Berman and Lonsdale, *Unhappy Valley*, p. 360.

39   Ngugi, *Detained*, p. 90.

40   Boehmer, 'The Master's Dance to the Master's Voice', pp. 192–3.

41   Judith Cochrane, 'Women as Guardians of the Tribe in Ngugi's Novels', in Killam (ed.), *Critical Perspectives on Ngugi wa Thiong'o*, p. 91.

42   *Ibid.*, p. 90.

43   Leslie Monkman, 'Kenya and the New Jerusalem in *A Grain of Wheat*', in Killam (ed.), *Critical Perspectives on Ngugi wa Thiong'o*, p. 212.

44   Carole Sicherman, 'Ngugi wa Thiong'o and the Writing of Kenyan History', *Research in African Literatures*, 20:3, Fall (1989).

45   Maughan Brown, *Land, Freedom and Fiction*, p. 254.

46   *Ibid.*, p. 254.

47   Ernest Renan, 'What is a nation?', in Bhabha (ed.), *Nation and Narration*, p. 11.

48   Fanon, *The Wretched of the Earth*, p. 136.

49   Nnolim, 'Structure and Theme in Ngugi wa Thiong'o's *A Grain of Wheat*', p. 217.

50   *Ibid.*, p. 217.

51   Bakhtin, *The Dialogic Imagination*, p. 411.

52   Fanon, *The Wretched of the Earth*, pp. 182–3.

Chapter 3

1   This will be addressed in the course of this chapter, and in greater detail in chapter 5.

2   George Santayana, *The Life of Reason* (London, 1905), p. 105.

3   Stuart Crehan, 'The Politics of the Signifier: Ngugi wa Thiong'o's *Petals of Blood*', in *World Literature Written in English*, 26:1 (1986), pp. 3–24.

4   Ngugi, *Barrel of a Pen* (Trenton N.J., African World Books, 1983), p. 90.

5   For further discussions of this, see Patrick Williams, 'Like Wounded Birds: Ngugi and the Intellectuals', *Yearbook of English Studies*, 27 (1997), and Carole Sichermann, 'Ngugi wa Thiong'o and the Writing of Kenyan History', *Research in African Literatures*, 20:3, Fall (1989).

6   The 'heap of footnotes' is a quote from Ngugi's essay 'Mau Mau is coming back' in *Barrel of a Pen*.

7   Florence Stratton, *African Literature and the Politics of Gender* (London, Routledge, 1994), p. 53.

8   *Ibid.*, p. 53.

9   Immanuel Wallerstein, *Historical Capitalism* (London, Verso, 1983), pp. 40, 101.

10 Marx, 'The Future Result of the British Rule in India', *Surveys from Exile: political writings* (Penguin, 1981), p. 325.

11 Terry Eagleton, *Walter Benjamin, or Towards a Revolutionary Criticism* (London, Verso, 1981), p. 73.

12 Ngugi and Micere Mugo, *The Trial of Dedan Kimathi* (London, Heinemann, 1976), pp. vii–viii.

13 Ian Henderson, *The Hunt for Kimathi* (London, Pan, 1962), p. 200.

14 *Ibid.*, p. 178.

15 Ngugi and Micere Mugo, *The Trial of Dedan Kimathi*, p. 73.

16 Stratton, *African Literature and the Politics of Gender*, p. 9.

17 Ingrid Bjorkman, *'Mother, Sing For Me': People's Theatre in Kenya* (London, Zed, 1989), p. 36.

18 Elleke Boehmer, 'The Master's Dance to the Master's Voice', *Journal of Commonwealth Literature*, 26:1 (1991), p. 189.

19 *Ibid.*, p. 195.

20 Slavoj Zizek, 'Multiculturalism, or the Cultural Logic of Multinational Capitalism', *New Left Review*, 225, Sept./Oct. (1997), pp. 28–51.

21 Ngugi, *Detained: A Writer's Prison Diary* (Oxford, Heinemann, 1981), p. xxi. It is interesting to note that Ngugi's opponents are here characterised, among other things, by 'abstract supernationalism', given both Fanon's insistence on the need to transcend the merely national level of struggle, and Ngugi's own growing espousal of a Pan-Africanist politics.

22 For a more extended discussion of intellectuals and activism in Ngugi's other works, see Williams, 'Like Wounded Birds: Ngugi and the Intellectuals', pp. 201–18.

23 Frantz Fanon, *The Wretched of the Earth* (Harmondsworth, Penguin, 1967), p. 178.

24 *Ibid.*, p. 179.

25 *Ibid.*, p. 180.

26   Bruce Berman and John Lonsdale, *Unhappy Valley* (London, James Currey, 1992), p. 298.

27   Sicherman, 'Ngugi wa Thiong'o and the Writing of Kenyan History'.

28   Robert Stamm, 'On the carnivalesque', *Wedge* (1, 1982), p. 55.

29   Gitahi Gititi, 'Recuperating a "Disappearing" Art Form: Resonances of "Gicaandi" in Ngugi wa Thiong'o's *Devil on the Cross*', in Cantalupo (ed.), *The World of Ngugi wa Thiong'o* (Trenton N.J., Africa World Press, 1995), pp. 122, 124.

30   Gayatri Spivak, *Outside in the Teaching Machine* (London, Routledge, 1992), p. 192.

31   Ngugi, *Detained*, p. 8.

32   Ngugi, *Decolonising the Mind* (London, James Currey, 1986), p. 16.

33   *Ibid.*, p. 78.

34   *Ibid.*, p. 103.

35   *Ibid.*, p. 29.

36   Ngugi and Ngugi wa Mirii, *I Will Marry When I Want* (London, Heinemann, 1982), pp. 113–14.

37   Edward Said, *Representations of the Intellectual* (London, Vintage, 1994), pp. 35, 43.

38   *Ibid.*, p. 45.

39   Ngugi, *Moving the Centre* (London, James Currey, 1993), p. 106.

40   *Ibid.*, p. 107.

41   Paolo Freire, *Pedagogy of the Oppressed* (London, Penguin, 1972).

42   Quoted in Edward Said, *The World, the Text and the Critic* (London, Faber, 1984), p. 80.

43   Ngugi, *Decolonising the Mind*, p. 183.

44   Ngugi, *Barrel of a Pen*, p. 41.

45   Ann Biersteker, '*Matigari ma Njiruungi*: What Grows from Leftover Seeds of "Chat" Trees?', in Cantalupo, *The World of Ngugi wa Thiong'o*, p. 142.

46   Ngugi, '*Matigari* as myth and history: an interview', *Third World Quarterly*, 11, 4, October 1989, p. 243.

47   Odun Balogun, 'Ngugi's *Matigari* and the Refiguration of the Novel as Genre', in Cantalupo (ed.), *The World of Ngugi wa Thiong'o*, p. 188.

48   *Ibid.*, p. 192.

49   Ian Adam and Helen Tiffin (eds), *Past the Last Post – Theorizing Post-Colonialism and Post-Modernism* (Hemel Hempstead, Harvester, 1991), p. x.

50   Ngugi, Interview, *Journal of Commonwealth Literature*, 21:1 (1986), p. 166.

51   Ngugi, *Moving the Centre*, pp. 109–10.

52   See, for example, Valentin Voloshinov, *Marxism and the Philosophy of Language* (Cambridge, Mass., Harvard University Press, 1986).

53   Said, *Representations of the Intellectual*, p. 65.

54   Mikhail Bakhtin, *The Dialogic Imagination* (Austin, University of Texas Press, 1981), p. 38.

55   Simon Gikandi, 'Ngugi's Conversion: Writing and the Politics of Language', *Research in African Literatures*, 23:1 (1992), p. 139.

56   Lewis Nkosi, 'Reading *Matigari*: The New Novel of Post-Independence', in Cantalupo, *The World of Ngugi wa Thiong'o*, p. 199.

57   Gikandi, 'Ngugi's Conversion', p. 139 (emphasis added).

58   Gadjigo *et al.* (eds), *Ousmane Sembene: Dialogues with Critics and Writers* (Amherst, University of Massachusetts Press, 1993), pp. 60–1.

59   Bob Hodge and Vijay Mishra, 'What is post(-)colonialism?', in Patrick Williams and Laura Chrisman (eds), *Colonial Discourse and Post-Colonial Theory* (Hemel Hempstead, Harvester Wheatsheaf, 1993), pp. 276–90.

60   Aijaz Ahmad, 'The Politics of Literary Postcoloniality', *Race and Class*, 36:3 (1995), p. 2.

61   Edward Said, *The Empire Writes Back* (London, Routledge, 1989).

Chapter 4

1   Ngugi, *Decolonising the Mind* (London, James Currey, 1986), p. 1.

2   Ngugi, 'Kenya: the Two Rifts', in *Homecoming* (London, Heinemann, 1972), p. 23.

3   Ngugi, 'Towards a National Culture', in *Homecoming*, p. 4.

4   Amilcar Cabral, 'Determined to resist', *Tricontinental*, 8 (1968).

5   Ngugi, 'Towards a National Culture' in *Homecoming*, p. 12.

6   *Ibid.*, p. 13.

7 Ngugi, 'Literature and Society', in *Writers in Politics* (London, Heinemann, 1981), p. 9.

8 *Ibid.*, p. 12.

9 *Ibid.*, p. 14.

10 *Ibid.*, p. 25.

11 Ngugi, 'Kenyan Culture: the National Struggle for Survival', in *Writers in Politics*, p. 42.

12 Ngugi, 'Education for a National Culture', in *Barrel of a Pen* (Trenton N.J., Africa World Books, 1983), p. 91.

13 *Ibid.*, p. 99.

14 Ngugi, 'The Universality of Local Knowledge', in *Moving the Centre* (London, James Currey, 1993), p. 25.

15 Ngugi, Preface to *Moving the Centre*, p. xvii.

16 Ngugi, 'Creating Space for a Hundred Flowers to Bloom', in *Moving the Centre*, p. 13.

17 Ngugi, 'Art War With the State', in *Penpoints, Gunpoints and Dreams* (Oxford, Clarendon Press, 1998), p. 8.

18 Ngugi, 'The Language of African Literature', in *Decolonising the Mind*, p. 15.

19 Modhumita Roy, 'Writers and Politics/Writers in Politics', in Charles Cantalupo (ed.), *Ngugi wa Thiong'o: Texts and Contexts* (Trenton N.J., Africa World Press, 1995), p. 68.

20 Ngugi, 'Towards a National Culture', in *Homecoming*, p. 16.

21 *Ibid.*, p. 19.

22 Obi Wali, *Transition*, 10 (1963).

23 Ngugi, 'Return to the Roots' in *Writers in Politics*, p. 59.

24 Ngugi, *Decolonising the Mind*, p. xiv.

25 Ngugi, 'The Language of African Literature', in *Decolonising the Mind*, p. 29.

26 Ngugi, 'Oral Power and Europhone Glory', in *Penpoints, Gunpoints and Dreams*, p. 127.

27 Joseph Mbele, 'Language in African Literature: An Aside to Ngugi', *Research in African Literatures*, 23:1 (1992), p. 145.

28 Simon Gikandi, 'Ngugi's Conversion: Writing and the Politics of Language', *Research in African Literatures*, 23:1 (1992), p. 132.

29 Ngugi, 'Return to the Roots', in *Writers in Politics*, p. 60.

30 Gikandi, 'Ngugi's Conversion', in *Writers in Politics*, p. 138.

31 *Ibid.*, p. 139.

32 Ngugi, 'The Language of African Literature', in *Decolonising the Mind*, p. 29.

33 Ngugi, 'Towards a National Culture', in *Homecoming*, p. 18.

34 Ngugi, 'The Writer and His Past', in *Homecoming*, p. 46.

35 Ngugi, Preface to *Writers in Politics*, p. xii.

36 Ngugi, 'Writers in Politics', in *Writers in Politics*, p. 79.

37 *Ibid.*, p. 80.

38 Ngugi, 'Freedom of the Artist', in *Barrel of a Pen*, p. 61.

39 *Ibid.*, p. 62.

40 Ngugi, 'Freedom of Expression', in *Writers in Politics* (Oxford, James Currey, revised edition, 1997), p. 81.

41 *Ibid.*, pp. 66–7.

42 Ngugi, *Detained: A Writer's Prison Diary* (Oxford, Heinemann, 1981), p. xxi.

43 Ngugi, 'Enactments of Power', in *Penpoints, Gunpoints and Dreams*, p. 60.

44 Ngugi, *Penpoints, Gunpoints and Dreams*, p. xi.

45 Ngugi, 'Enactments of Power', in *Penpoints, Gunpoints and Dreams*, p. 38.

46 Ngugi, 'In Moi's Kenya, History is Subversive', in *Moving the Centre*, p. 96.

47 *Ibid.*, p. 100.

48 Ngugi, 'Learning from our Ancestors', in *Writers in Politics*, p. 139.

49 *Ibid.*, p. 151.

50 *Ibid.*, p. 149.

51 Ngugi, 'Matigari and the Dreams of one East Africa', in *Moving the Centre*, p. 169.

52 Ngugi, 'The Cultural Factor in the Neo-Colonial Era', in *Moving the Centre*, p. 56.

53 *Ibid.*, p. 57.

54 Martin Carter, 'Looking at your hands', in *Poems of Succession* (London, New Beacon Books, 1977), p. 14.

Chapter 5

1   Carole Sicherman, *Ngugi wa Thiong'o: A Bibliography of Primary and Secondary Sources 1957–1987* (London, Hans Zell, 1989).

2   John Updike, 'Mixed Reports from the Interior', *New Yorker*, 2:7 (1979), pp. 91–4.

3   David Maughan Brown, *Land, Freedom and Fiction: History and Ideology in Kenya* (London, Zed, 1985), p. 256.

4   C. B. Robson, *Ngugi wa Thiong'o* (London, Macmillan, 1979), p. 129.

5   *Ibid.*, p. 101.

6   *Ibid.*, p. 131.

7   *Ibid.*, p. 139.

8   Andrew Gurr, 'The Fourth Novel: Ngugi's *Petals of Blood*', in Jefferson and Martin (eds), *The Uses of Fiction* (Milton Keynes, Open University Press, 1982).

9   G. D. Killam, *An Introduction to the Writings of Ngugi* (London, Heinemann, 1980).

10   *Ibid.*, p. 115.

11   David Cook and Michael Okenimkpe, *Ngugi wa Thiong'o: An Exploration of His Writings* (Oxford, James Currey, second edition 1997), p. 104.

12   *Ibid.*, p. 98.

13   Ngugi, *Petals of Blood* (Oxford, Heinemann, 1977), p. 333.

14   Simon Gikandi, *Reading the African Novel* (London, James Currey, 1987), p. 146.

15   Stuart Crehan, 'The Politics of the Signifier: Ngugi wa Thiong'o's *Petals of Blood*' in *World Literature Written in English* 26:1 (1986), p. 1.

16   *Ibid.*, p. 1.

17   *Ibid.*, p. 12.

18   Mikhail Bakhtin, *The Dialogic Imagination* (Austin, University of Texas Press, 1981), p. 293.

19   Crehan, 'The Politics of the Signifier: Ngugi wa Thiong'o's *Petals of Blood*', pp. 6–7.

20   *Ibid.*, p. 6.

21   Cook and Okenimkpe, *Ngugi wa Thiong'o: An Exploration of His Writings*, p. 107.

22 *Ibid.*, pp. 101–2.

23 Lisa Curtis, 'The Divergence of Art and Ideology in the Later Novels of Ngugi wa Thiong'o: A Critique', in *Ufahamu: Journal of the African Activists Association*, 13, 2–3 (1984), p. 188.

24 *Ibid.*, p. 199.

25 *Ibid.*, p. 187.

26 *Ibid.*, pp. 197–8.

27 Ngugi, *Petals of Blood*, p. 68.

28 Curtis, 'The Divergence of Art and Ideology', pp. 198–9.

29 Ngugi, *Barrel of a Pen* (Trenton N.J., Africa World Books, 1983), pp. 59–60.

30 Curtis, 'The Divergence of Art and Ideology', p. 204.

31 *Ibid.*, p. 206.

32 Grant Kamenju, '*Petals of Blood* as a Mirror of the African Revolution', in George Gugelberger (ed.), *Marxism and African Literature* (London, James Currey, 1985).

33 Peter Nazareth, 'The Second Homecoming: Multiple Ngugis in *Petals of Blood*', in Gugelberger (ed.), *Marxism and African Literature*.

34 Alamin Mazrui and Lupenga Mphande, *Ufahamu*, 18:2 (1990), p. 49.

35 Carole Sicherman, 'Ngugi wa Thiong'o and the Writing of Kenyan History', *Research in African Literatures*, 20:3, Fall (1989), p. 360.

36 Ngugi, *Petals of Blood*, p. 67.

37 Bruce Berman and John Lonsdale, *Unhappy Valley* (London, James Currey, 1992), p. 298.

38 Walter Benjamin, 'Theses on the Philosophy of History', in *Illuminations* (London, Fontana, 1973), p. 259.

39 *Ibid.*, p. 257.

Select bibliography

Works by Ngugi

NOVELS

Weep Not, Child, Oxford, Heinemann, 1964.
The River Between, Oxford, Heinemann, 1965.
A Grain of Wheat, Oxford, Heinemann, 1967.
Petals of Blood, Oxford, Heinemann, 1977.
Devil on the Cross, Oxford, Heinemann, 1982.
Matigari, Oxford, Heinemann, 1987.

PLAYS

The Black Hermit, Oxford, Heinemann, 1968.
The Trial of Dedan Kimathi, Oxford, Heinemann, 1976.
I Will Marry When I Want, Oxford, Heinemann, 1982.

SHORT STORIES

Secret Lives, Oxford, Heinemann, 1975.

ESSAYS

Homecoming, London, Heinemann, 1972.
Writers in Politics, London, Heinemann, 1981.
Detained: A Writer's Prison Diary, Oxford, Heinemann, 1981.
Barrel of a Pen, Trenton N.J., Africa World Books, 1983.
Decolonising the Mind, London, James Currey, 1986.

Moving the Centre, London, James Currey, 1993.

Writers in Politics (revised edition), Oxford, James Currey, 1997.

Penpoints, Gunpoints and Dreams, Oxford, Clarendon Press, 1998.

CHILDREN'S BOOKS

Njamba Nene and the Flying Bus, Nairobi, Heinemann, 1986. (Translation by Wangui wa Goro of *Njamba Nene na Mbaathi i Mathagu*, 1982)

Njamba Nene's Pistol, Nairobi, Heinemann, 1986. (Translation by Wangui wa Goro of *Baithoora ya Njamba Nene*, 1984)

Selected interviews

Interviews with Dennis Duerden and Aminu Abdullahi, in Duerden and Pieterse, eds., *African Writers Talking*, New York, Africana Publishing, 1972, pp. 121–31.

'Interview with Ngugi wa Thiong'o', Jurgen Martini *et al.*, *Kunapipi*, 3:1 (1981), pp. 110–16.

'Ngugi wa Thiong'o', interview with Ingrid Bjorkman, *Kunapipi*, 4:2 (1982), pp. 126–34.

'An Interview with Ngugi wa Thiong'o', Bettye J. Parker, in Killam, G. D. (ed.), *Critical Perspectives on Ngugi wa Thiong'o* (Washington, Three Continents Press, 1984), pp. 58–66.

'A Political Choice', interview with Kwesi Owusu, *West Africa*, 18–8–1986, pp. 1734–5.

'Ngugi wa Thiong'o – interviewed by Hansel Nolumbe Eyoh', *Journal of Commonwealth Literature*, 23:1 (1986), pp. 162–6.

'*Matigari* as myth and history: an interview', *Third World Quarterly*, 11:4 (1989), pp. 241–51.

'Ngugi wa Thiong'o', in Jussawalla, F., and Dasenbrook, R. W. (eds), *Interviews with Writers of the Post-Colonial World* (Jackson and London, University of Mississippi Press, 1995), pp. 24–41.

Selected criticism on Ngugi

Afejuku, T., 'Autobiography as History and Political Testament: Ngugi wa Thiong'o's *Detained*', *World Literature Written in English*, 30:1 (1990), pp. 78–87.

Amuta, C., 'The Revolutionary Imperative in the Contemporary African Novel: Ngugi's *Petals of Blood* and Armah's *The Healers*', *Commonwealth Novel in English*, 3:2 (1990), pp. 130–42.

Biersteker, A., '*Matigari ma Njiruungi*: What Grows from Leftover Seeds of "Chat" Trees?', in Cantalupo (ed.), *The World of Ngugi wa Thiong'o* (Trenton N.J., Africa World Press, 1995), pp. 141–58.

Bjorkman, I., '*Mother, Sing For Me*': People's Theatre in Kenya (London, Zed Press, 1989).

Boehmer, E., 'The Master's Dance to the Master's Voice', *Journal of Commonwealth Literature*, 26:1 (1991), pp. 188–97.

Cantalupo, C. (ed.), *Ngugi wa Thiong'o: Texts and Contexts* (Trenton N.J., Africa World Press, 1995).

Cantalupo, C. (ed.), *The World of Ngugi wa Thiong'o* (Trenton N.J., Africa World Press, 1995).

Carter, S., 'Decolonization and Detective Fiction: Ngugi wa Thiong'o's *Petals of Blood*', *Clues: A Journal of Detection*, 8:1 (1987), pp. 101–26.

Cochrane, J., 'Women as Guardians of the Tribe in Ngugi's Novels', in Killam (ed.), *Critical Perspectives on Ngugi wa Thiong'o*, pp. 90–100.

Cook, D., and Okenimkpe, M., *Ngugi wa Thiong'o: An Exploration of His Writings* (Oxford, James Currey, second edition, 1997).

Crehan, S., 'The Politics of the Signifier: Ngugi wa Thiong'o's *Petals of Blood*', *World Literature Written in English*, 26:1 (1986), pp. 1–24.

Curtis, L., 'The Divergence of Art and Ideology in the Later Novels of Ngugi wa Thiong'o: A Critique', *Ufahamu*, 13, 2–3 (1984), pp. 186–214.

Gikandi, S., 'On Culture and State: The Writings of Ngugi wa Thiong'o', *Third World Quarterly*, 11:1 (1989), pp. 148–56.

Gikandi, S., 'Ngugi's Conversion: Writing and the Politics of Language', *Research in African Literatures*, 23:1 (1992), pp. 131–44.

Gititi, G., 'Recuperating a "Disappearing" Art Form: Resonances of "Gicaandi" in Ngugi wa Thiong'o's *Devil on the Cross*', in Cantalupo (ed.), *The World of Ngugi wa Thiong'o*, pp. 109–28.

Glinga, W., 'The River Between and its Forerunners', World Literature Written in English, 26:2 (1986), pp. 211–28.

Gurnah, A., 'Matigari: A Tract of Resistance', Research in African Literatures, 22:4 (1991), pp. 169–72.

Gurr, A., 'The Fourth Novel: Ngugi's Petals of Blood', in Jefferson and Martin (eds), The Uses of Fiction (Milton Keynes, Open University Press, 1982), pp. 159–70.

Harrow, K., 'Ngugi wa Thiong'o's A Grain of Wheat: Season of Irony', Research in African Literatures, 16:2 (1985), pp. 243–63.

Indangasi, H., 'Ngugi's Ideal Reader and the Postcolonial Reality', in Yearbook of English Studies, 27 (1997), pp. 193–200.

Jabbi, B-B., 'The Structure of Symbolism in A Grain of Wheat', Research in African Literatures, 16:2 (1985), pp. 210–42.

Jussawalla, F., 'The Language of Struggle: Ngugi wa Thiong'o on the Prisonhouse of Language', Transition, 54 (1991), pp. 142–54.

Kamenju, G., 'Petals of Blood as a Mirror of the African Revolution', in Gugelberger (ed.), Marxism and African Literature (London, James Currey, 1985), pp. 130–5.

Killam, G. D., Introduction to the Writings of Ngugi (London, Heinemann, 1980).

Killam, G. D. (ed.), Critical Perspectives on Ngugi wa Thiong'o (Washington, Three Continents Press, 1984).

Last, B. W., 'Ngugi and Soyinka: An Ideological Contrast', World Literature Written in English, 21:3 (1982), pp. 510–21.

Lazarus, N., '(Re)turn to the People: Ngugi wa Thiong'o and the Crisis of Postcolonial Intellectualism', in Cantalupo (ed.), The World of Ngugi wa Thiong'o, pp. 11–25.

Lindfors, B., 'Ngugi's early journalism', World Literature Written in English, 20:1 (1981), pp. 23–41.

Massa, D., 'The Post–Colonial Dream', World Literature Written in English, 20:1 (1981), pp. 135–49.

Maughan Brown, D., 'Matigari and the Rehabilitation of Religion', Research in African Literatures, 22:4 (1991), pp. 173–80.

Mazrui, A., and Mphande, L., 'The Historical Imperative in African Activist Literature', Ufahamu, 18:2 (1990), pp. 47–58.

Mbele, J., 'Language in African Literature: an aside to Ngugi', Research in African Literatures, 23:1 (1992), pp. 145–51.

Monkman, L., 'Kenya and the New Jerusalem in A Grain of Wheat', in

Killam (ed.), *Critical Perspectives on Ngugi wa Thiong'o*.

Nama, C., 'Daughters of Moombi: Ngugi's Heroines and Traditional Gikuyu Aesthetics', in Davies, C. B., and Graves, A. A. (eds), *Ngambika: Studies of Women in African Literature* (Trenton, N.J., Africa World Press, 1986), pp. 139–49.

Nazareth, P., 'The Second Homecoming: Multiple Ngugis in *Petals of Blood*', in Gugelberger (ed.), *Marxism and African Literature*, pp. 118–29.

Nkosi, L., 'Reading *Matigari*: The New Novel of Post–Independence', in Cantalupo (ed.), *The World of Ngugi wa Thiong'o*, pp. 197–206.

Nnolim, C., 'Structure and Theme in Ngugi wa Thiong'o's *A Grain of Wheat*', in Killam (ed.), *Critical Perspectives on Ngugi wa Thiong'o*, pp. 217–30.

Nwankwo, C., 'Women in Ngugi's Plays: From Passivity to Social Responsibility', *Ufahamu*, 14:2 (1985), pp. 85–92.

Odun Balogun, F., 'Ngugi's *Matigari* and the Refiguration of the Novel as Genre', in Cantalupo (ed.), *The World of Ngugi wa Thiong'o*, pp. 185–96.

Pagnoulle, C., 'Ngugi wa Thiong'o's "Journey of the Magi": Part 2 of *Petals of Blood*', *Research in African Literatures*, 16:2 (1985), pp. 264–75.

Petersen, K. H., 'Birth Pangs of a National Consciousness: Mau Mau and Ngugi wa Thiong'o', *World Literature Written in English*, 20:2 (1981), pp. 214–19.

Reed, J., 'Decolonising the Mind', *World Literature Written in English*, 27:2 (1987), pp. 215–28.

Riemenschneider, D., 'Ngugi wa Thiong'o and the Question of Language and Literature in Kenya', *World Literature Written in English*, 24:1 (1984), pp. 78–87.

Robson, C. B., *Ngugi wa Thiong'o* (London, Macmillan, 1979).

Roy, M., 'Writers and Politics / Writers in Politics', in Cantalupo (ed.), *Ngugi wa Thiong'o: Texts and Contexts* (Trenton N.J., Africa World Press, 1995), pp. 165–86.

Schwerdt, D., 'Deconstructing Cultural Imperialism: African Literature and the Politics of Language', *Southern Review*, 24:1 (1991), pp. 57–68.

Sekyi-Otu, A., 'The Refusal of Agency: The Founding Narrative and Waiyaki's Tragedy in *The River Between*', *Research in African Literatures*, 16:2 (1985), pp. 157–78.

Sharma, G. N., 'Ngugi's Apocalypse: Marxism, Christianity and African Utopianism in *Petals of Blood*', *World Literature Written in English*, 18:1 (1979), pp. 77–91.

Sharma, G. N., 'Ngugi's Christian Vision: Theme and Pattern in *A Grain of Wheat*', in Killam, G. D. (ed.), *Critical Perspectives on Ngugi wa Thiong'o*, pp. 201–10.

Sicherman, C., *Ngugi wa Thiong'o: A Bibliography of Primary and Secondary Sources 1957–1987* (London, Hans Zell, 1989).

Sicherman, C., 'Ngugi wa Thiong'o and the Writing of Kenyan History', *Research in African Literatures*, 20:3, Fall (1989), pp. 347–70.

Sicherman, C., *Ngugi wa Thiong'o: The Making of a Rebel* (London, Hans Zell, 1990).

Updike, J., 'Mixed Reports from the Interior', *New Yorker*, 2–7–1979, pp. 91–4.

Wamalwa, D. S., 'The Engaged Artist: The Social Vision of Ngugi wa Thiong'o', *Africa Today*, 33:1 (1986), pp. 9–18.

Williams, K., 'Decolonising the Word: Language, Culture, and Self in the Works of Ngugi wa Thiong'o and Gabriel Okara', *Research in African Literatures*, 22:4 (1991), pp. 53–61.

Williams, P., 'Like Wounded Birds: Ngugi and the Intellectuals', *Yearbook of English Studies*, 27 (1997), pp. 201–18.

Wise, C., 'Resurrecting the Devil: Notes on Ngugi's Theory of the Oral-Aural African Novel', *Research in African Literatures*, 28:1 (1997), pp. 134–40.

General criticism and theory

Achebe, C., *Hopes and Impediments: Selected Essays 1965–87* (Oxford, Heinemann, 1988).

Adam, I., and Tiffin, H. (eds), *Past the Last Post – Theorizing Post-Colonialism and Post-Modernism* (Hemel Hempstead, Harvester, 1991).

Agovi, K. E., 'The African Writer and the Phenomenon of the Nation State in Africa', *Ufahamu*, 18:1 (1990), pp. 41–62.

Ahmad, A., *In Theory: Classes, Nations, Literatures* (London, Verso, 1992).

Ahmad, A., 'The Politics of Literary Postcoloniality', *Race and Class*, 36:3 (1995).

Althusser, L., 'Ideology and Ideological State Apparatuses', in *Essays on Ideology* (London, Verso, 1984).

Amuta, C., *The Theory of African Literature* (London, Zed, 1989).

Anderson, B., *Imagined Communities* (London, Verso, 1983).

Bakhtin, M., *The Dialogic Imagination* (Austin, University of Texas Press, 1981).

Benjamin, W., 'Theses on the Philosophy of History', in *Illuminations* (London, Fontana, 1973).

Berman, B., and Lonsdale, J., *Unhappy Valley* (London, James Currey, 1992).

Bhabha, H. K. (ed.), *Nation and Narration* (London, Routledge, 1990).

Boehmer, E., *Colonial and Postcolonial Literature* (Oxford, Oxford University Press, 1995).

Césaire, A., *Discourse on Colonialism* (New York, Monthly Review Press, 1972).

Childs, P., and Williams, P., *Introduction to Post-Colonial Theory* (Hemel Hempstead, Harvester/Prentice Hall, 1996).

Davidson, B., *The Black Man's Burden: Africa and the Curse of the Nation-State* (London, James Currey, 1992).

Davies, C. B., and Graves, A. A. (eds), *Ngambika: Studies of Women in African Literature* (Trenton, N.J., Africa World Press, 1986).

Eagleton, T., *Walter Benjamin, or Towards a Revolutionary Criticism* (London, Verso, 1981).

Fanon, F., *The Wretched of the Earth* (Harmondsworth, Penguin, 1967).

Foucault, M., *History of Sexuality*, Vol. 1 (Harmondsworth, Penguin, 1981).

Furedi, F., *Colonial Wars and the Politics of Third World Nationalism* (London, I. B. Tauris, 1994).

Furedi, F., *The New Ideology of Imperialism* (London, Pluto, 1994).

Gadjigo, S. *et al.* (eds), *Ousmane Sembene: Dialogues with Critics and Writers* (Amherst, University of Massachusetts Press, 1993).

Gikandi, S., *Reading the African Novel* (London, James Currey, 1987).

Gugelberger, G. (ed.), *Marxism and African Literature* (London, James Currey, 1985).

Harlow, B., *Resistance Literature* (London, Methuen, 1987).

Harrow, K., *Thresholds of Change in African Literature* (London, James Currey, 1993).

Hobsbawm, E., and Ranger, T., *The Invention of Tradition* (Cambridge, Cambridge University Press, 1983).

Jameson, F., *The Political Unconscious* (London, Methuen, 1981).

Jameson, F., 'Third World Literature in the Era of Multinational Capitalism', *Social Text*, Fall (1986), pp. 65–88.

JanMohamed, A., *Manichean Aesthetics* (Amherst, University of Massachusetts Press, 1983).

Kenyatta, J., *Facing Mount Kenya* (Oxford, Heinemann, 1979).

Lazarus, N., *Resistance in Postcolonial African Fiction* (New Haven, Yale University Press, 1990).

Maina wa Kinyatti (ed.), *Thunder From the Mountains* (London, Zed Press, 1980).

Maughan Brown, D., *Land, Freedom and Fiction: History and Ideology in Kenya* (London, Zed, 1985).

Mazrui, A., 'Ideology or Pedagogy: the Linguistic Indigenisation of African Literature', *Race and Class*, 28:1 (1986), pp. 63–72.

Msiska, M-H., and Hyland, P. (eds), *Writing and Africa* (London, Longman, 1997).

Neale, C., *Writing 'Independent' History: African Historiography 1960–1980* (Stanford, Stanford University Press, 1985).

Ngara, E., *Art and Ideology in the African Novel* (London, Heinemann, 1985).

Nkosi, L., *Tasks and Masks: Themes and Styles of African Literature* (Harlow, Longman, 1981).

Nnaemeka, O., *The Politics of (M)Othering* (London, Routledge, 1997).

Rodney, W., *How Europe Underdeveloped Africa* (London, Bogle L'Ouverture, 1988).

Said, E., *The World, the Text and the Critic* (London, Faber, 1984).

Said, E., *Culture and Imperialism* (London, Chatto & Windus, 1993).

Said, E., *Representations of the Intellectual* (London, Vintage, 1994).

Spivak, G., *Outside in the Teaching Machine* (London, Routledge, 1992).

Stratton, F., *African Literature and the Politics of Gender* (London, Routledge, 1994).

Voloshinov, V., *Marxism and the Philosophy of Language* (Cambridge, Mass., Harvard University Press, 1986).

Wallerstein, I., *Historical Capitalism* (London, Verso, 1983).

Williams, P., and Chrisman, L. (eds), *Colonial Discourse and Post-Colonial Theory* (Hemel Hempstead, Harvester Wheatsheaf, 1993).

Zizek, S., 'Multiculturalism, or the Cultural Logic of Multinational Capitalism', *New Left Review*, 225, Sept./Oct. (1997).

Index